THE
ART OF
CELTIA

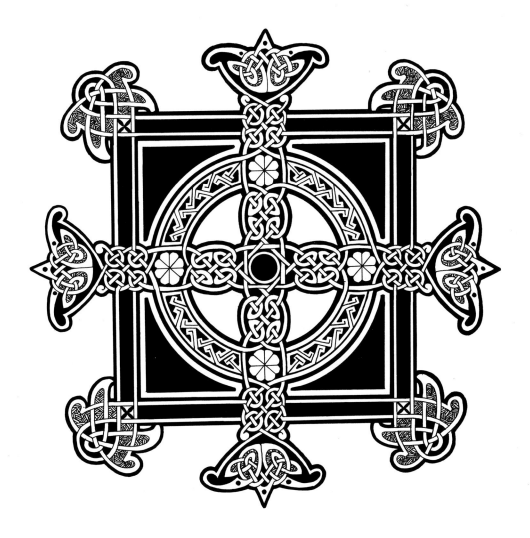

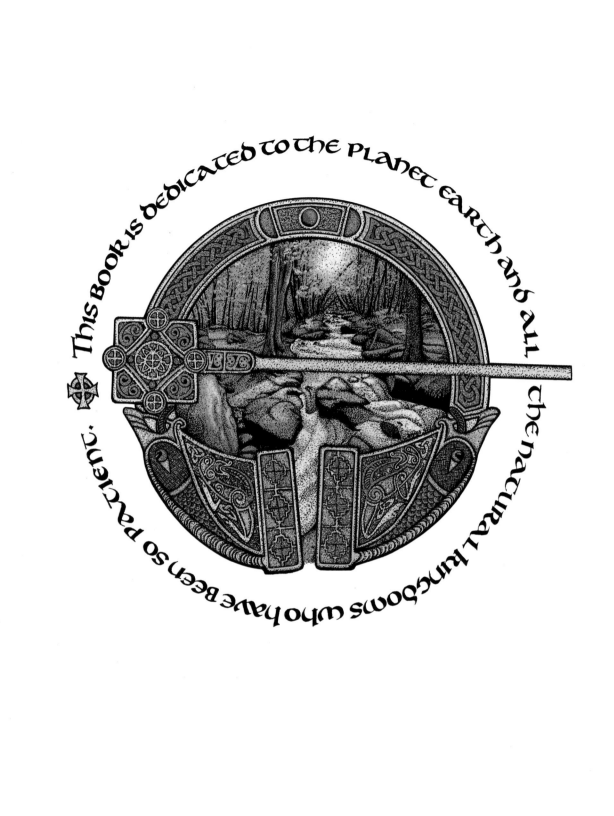

THIS BOOK IS DEDICATED TO THE PLANET EARTH AND ALL THE NATURAL KINGDOMS WHO HAVE BEEN SO PATIENT.

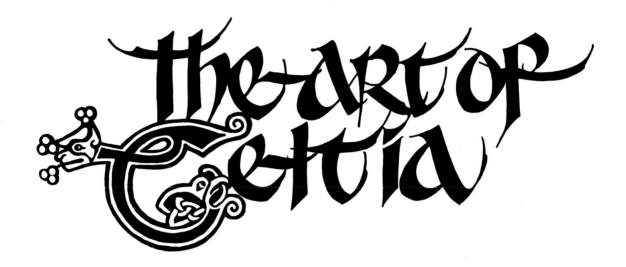

THE ART OF CELTIA

COURTNEY DAVIS

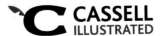

CASSELL
ILLUSTRATED

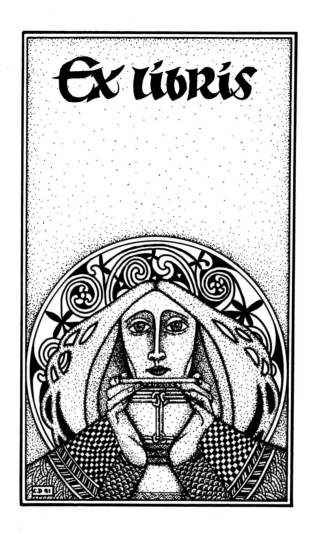

A BLANDFORD BOOK
This paperback edition first published in the UK in 1994
by Blandford, a Cassell imprint
Cassell Illustrated 2-4 Heron Quays, London E 14 4 JB
Reprinted 1995, 1996, 1997, 1998, 2000, 2002

Illustrations & text copyright © 1993 and 1995 Spirit of Celtia Ltd

Distributed in the United States by Sterling Publishing Co., Inc.
387 Park Avenue South, New York, NY 10016–8810

A catalogue entry for this title is available from the British Library

ISBN 0-7137-2307-6

Typeset by Litho Link Ltd, Welshpool, Powys, Wales
Printed and bound in Spain

CONTENTS

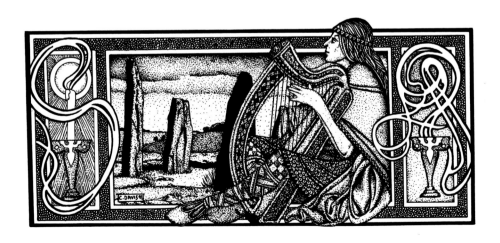

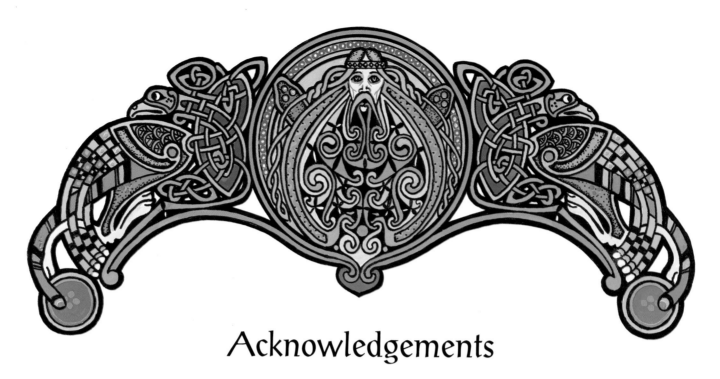

Acknowledgements

The following writers and publishers have kindly allowed me to use various pieces of text and illustrations in this book: Eleanor C. Merry, *The Flaming Door*: Floris Books; Robert Van de Weyer, *Celtic Fire*: Doubleday; John Matthews, *Taliesin:* Aquarian; Alexander Carmichael, *Carmina Gadelica*: Scottish Academic Press; Peter Quiller and Courtney Davis, *Merlin the Immortal*: Spirit of Celtia; Peter Quiller and Courtney Davis, *Merlin Awakes*: Firebird Books; Forrester Roberts and Courtney Davis, *Symbols of the Grail Quest*: Spirit of Celtia; Nigel Pennick, *Celtic Art in the Northern Tradition*: Nideck; Ronan Coghlan, *The Encyclopedia of Arthurian Legends*: Element Books; Steve Blamires, *The Irish Celtic Magical Tradition*: Aquarian; Bob Stewart, *Celtic Gods, Celtic Goddesses*: Blandford; John Sharkey, *Celtic Mysteries*, Thames and Hudson.

I should like to thank Dimity Taiani for her patience and love over this period of great change, and Chris Roberts firstly for his friendship and secondly for his additional text throughout the book.

I should also like to thank Ayliffe Davis, Lynne Brown, Helena Patterson, Sue and Pete Riddle, Mick Sawtell, John and Caitlin Matthews, Bob Stewart, Johan Quanjer, Peter Quiller, Steve Blamires and Sue, Sir George Trevelyan, and many others too numerous to include who have supported and encouraged me over the last few years.

'The Scribe' (1992)

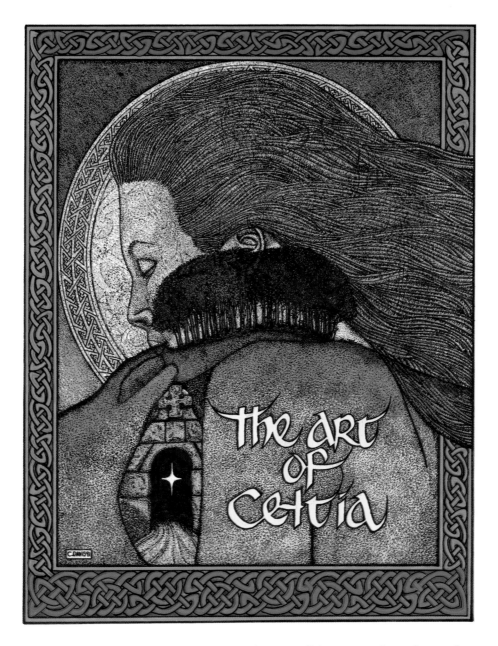

My hand is weary from writing; my sharp quill is not steady, as its tender tip spits its dark blue stream, the words which are formed on the page are jagged and uncertain.

O Lord may it be your wisdom, not my folly, which passes through my arm and hand, may it be your words that take shape upon the page. For when I am truly faithful to your dedication, my hand is firm and strong. Let me never write words that are callous or profane, let your priceless jewels shine upon these pages.

From *Celtic Fire*

'The Art of Celtia' (1991)

7

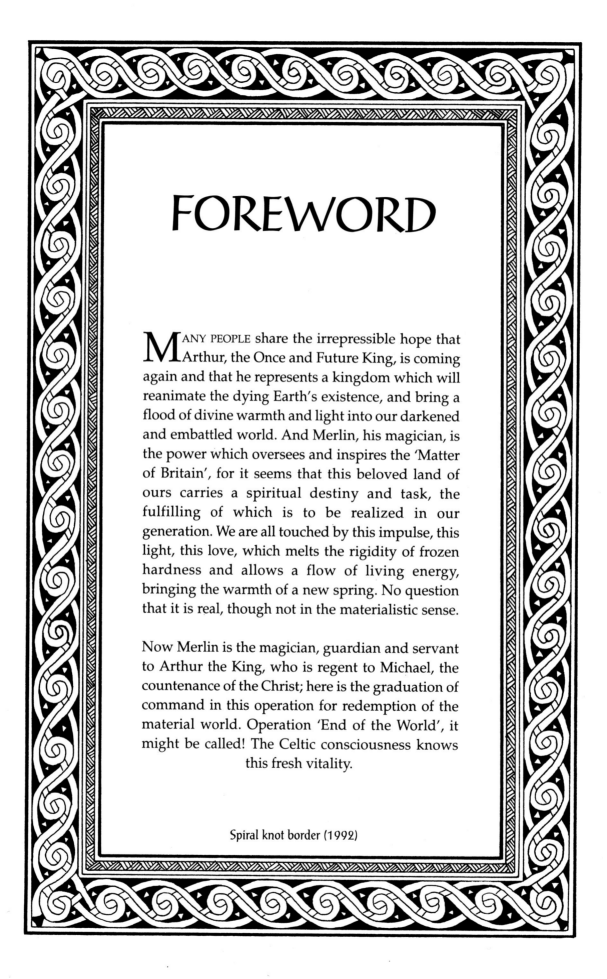

FOREWORD

MANY PEOPLE share the irrepressible hope that Arthur, the Once and Future King, is coming again and that he represents a kingdom which will reanimate the dying Earth's existence, and bring a flood of divine warmth and light into our darkened and embattled world. And Merlin, his magician, is the power which oversees and inspires the 'Matter of Britain', for it seems that this beloved land of ours carries a spiritual destiny and task, the fulfilling of which is to be realized in our generation. We are all touched by this impulse, this light, this love, which melts the rigidity of frozen hardness and allows a flow of living energy, bringing the warmth of a new spring. No question that it is real, though not in the materialistic sense.

Now Merlin is the magician, guardian and servant to Arthur the King, who is regent to Michael, the countenance of the Christ; here is the graduation of command in this operation for redemption of the material world. Operation 'End of the World', it might be called! The Celtic consciousness knows this fresh vitality.

Spiral knot border (1992)

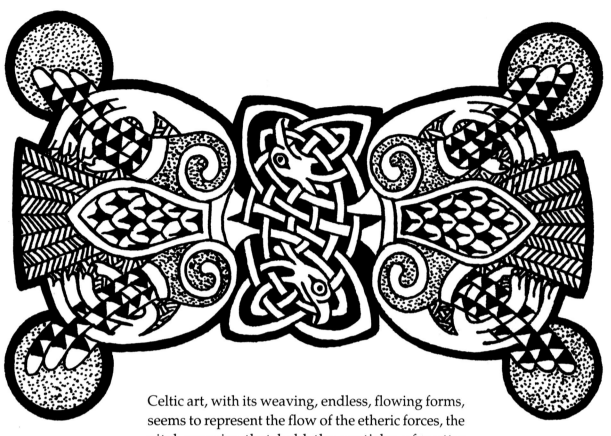

Celtic art, with its weaving, endless, flowing forms, seems to represent the flow of the etheric forces, the vital energies that hold the particles of matter together. The 'wild hope' of the coming of Arthur and Merlin, obstinately held somewhere in our consciousness, represents this impulse, which is truth. In our age, an energy which is life/light/love floods the Earth, reanimating the realm of matter. So high is the frequency of the field that it will repel all particles and beings vibrating on the low frequency of egoism, greed, getting for self, violence, hate, rivalry and war. It will reject and repel and throw out such elements. This could happen 'in the twinkling of an eye'. 'And this mortal shall put on incorruption and this mortal shall put on immortality and we shall all be changed.' Crisis and cataclysm in our time means opportunity and transformation. Glory be!

Celtic bird motifs (1992)

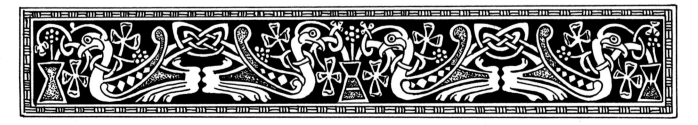

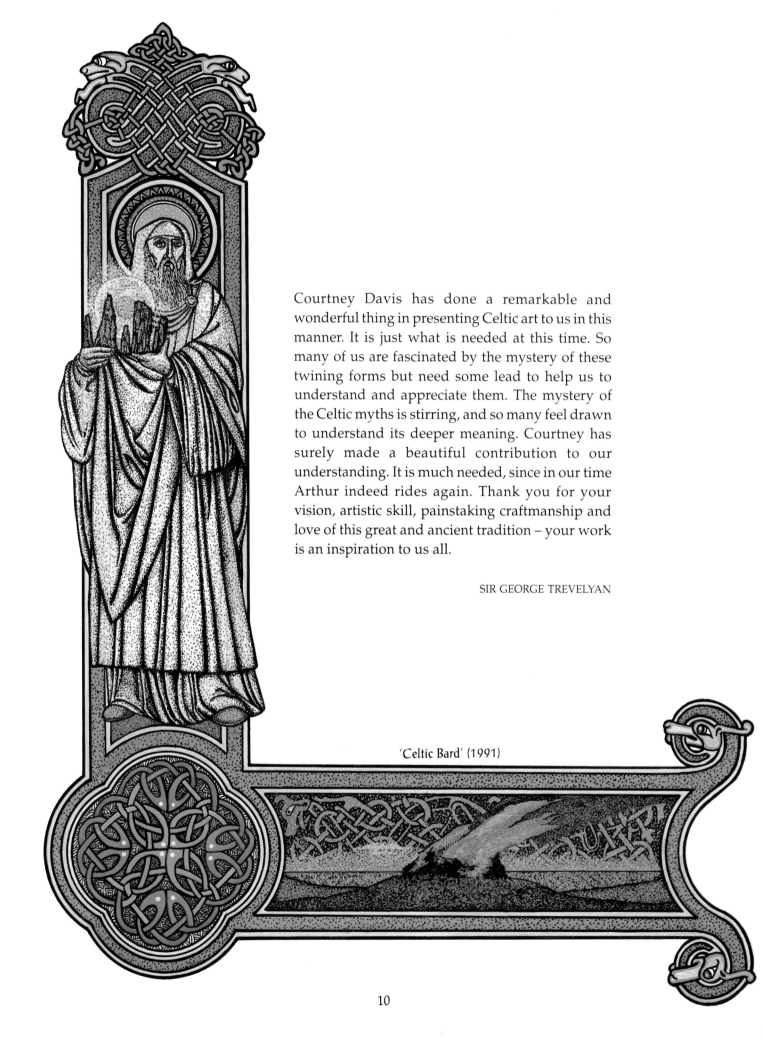

Courtney Davis has done a remarkable and wonderful thing in presenting Celtic art to us in this manner. It is just what is needed at this time. So many of us are fascinated by the mystery of these twining forms but need some lead to help us to understand and appreciate them. The mystery of the Celtic myths is stirring, and so many feel drawn to understand its deeper meaning. Courtney has surely made a beautiful contribution to our understanding. It is much needed, since in our time Arthur indeed rides again. Thank you for your vision, artistic skill, painstaking craftmanship and love of this great and ancient tradition – your work is an inspiration to us all.

SIR GEORGE TREVELYAN

'Celtic Bard' (1991)

THE FLAMING DOOR

THERE IS, stirring beneath the surface of things, a secret urge towards the establishment of a new spirit – a desire for the birth of a purely external political 'Celticism'. But this would only fall into line with much that is spiritually retrograde in our modern civilization. The old gods can no longer be invoked with impunity; the folk-souls of the past have another mission today. Men are afraid of the real future, and seek refuge amongst the phantoms of other ages, into which they breathe the breath of their desire.

And this is the other pole: the Celtic folk-soul is no longer the soul of a people, but the soul of a spiritual awakening of mankind. The blue mantle of St Bride is her banner shaken out over the expectant heavens. 'King Arthur' will not be roused by the blast of the horn of any national egotism, though it may shake the Earth; he will awaken only at the touch of the 'Woman of Beauty' who will 'come into the hearts of men and women like flame upon dry grass, like a flame of wind in a great wood'.

'St Patrick' (1991)

11

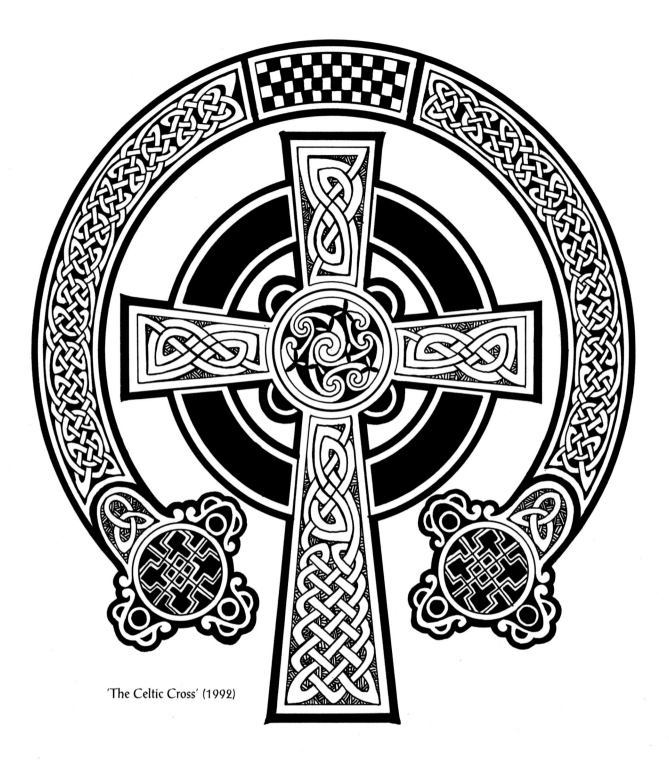

'The Celtic Cross' (1992)

The Celtic Mysteries of old are the signature of our immortality. They are the ladder upon which Christian faith may mount to the stars. The Celtic Spirit that prepared the way for the Holy Grail is the forerunner of all the Announcers of Christ, whose great procession will *follow* His 'second coming', when He is admitted at last into the hearts of the nation-souls of the world. In no external way should we dare to call this Celtic Spirit down into the councils of humanity, but only as a spiritual fertilizing power.

From *The Flaming Door*

God

I am the wind that breathes upon the sea,
I am the wave on the ocean,
I am the murmur of the leaves rustling,
I am the rays of the sun,
I am the beam of the moon and stars,
I am the power of trees growing,

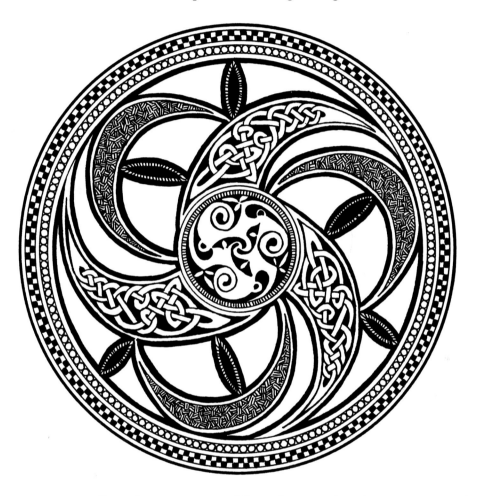

I am the movement of the salmon swimming,
I am the courage of the wild boar fighting,
I am the speed of the stag running,
I am the strength of the ox pulling the plough,
I am the size of the mighty oak tree,
And I am the thoughts of all people
Who praise my beauty and grace.

From *Celtic Fire*

'The Moving Spiral' (1992)
based on the Phoenix Park openwork mount, 8th century

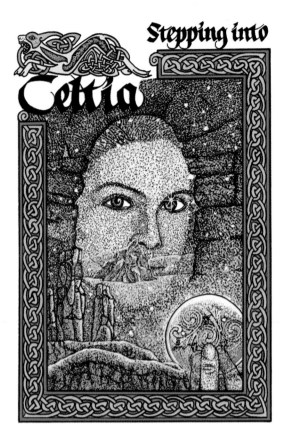

Stepping into Celtia

Cover of the Celtia catalogue

THE SACRED PRESENCE

Please don't underestimate the importance of an awareness of what lies beneath the surface of the visible world and of those ancient, unconscious forces which still help to shape the psychological attitudes of modern man.

HRH THE PRINCE OF WALES

From the beginnings of human life on this Earth, mankind has needed to express the feeling of the sacred that dwelt within him. In each age, with its greater knowledge of the existence of higher dimensions, the increasingly sophisticated symbolism that was employed reflected this new understanding. The persistence of this urge showed in every artistic medium from paintings to metal work and stone work, in artefacts of sometimes awesome beauty.

Many of us nowadays have divorced ourselves from Life – we have removed the spiritual from nature in a civilization that poisons the natural resources that our material as well as our spiritual wellbeing depend upon, because we do not see nature or any condition of it as sacred. The equilibrium between the spiritual and the material worlds is out of balance and so in turn are we.

Through my work with its complex weaving patterns and ancient natural symbolism I am rediscovering for myself a meaning to my own identity and my path and place in the great universal pattern that binds us and everything around us together. In the solitude and struggle, as I work on the paintings I attempt to unlock a sense of the mystery of the universe itself and bring my feelings of wonder at it to life.

It was through the death of my father that I found time to stop and think of my future. This was the time that I first began to draw again after a gap of many years. I found that expresssing myself through art could appease the hurt. Yet it was no mere therapy – something had changed. Now, I did not have to compose the picture in my head before starting to draw. Anything that I consciously tried to fit into the work was discarded; the picture would not flow until any preconceived idea was removed. I sensed I was being given a compelling sense of direction in the way that I worked. It was only after having painted my first series of images in this way that I became aware that they contained some of the oldest Western sacred symbols, and were in fact pictures unconsciously inspired by the culture of the Celts. I had to be told this. I have worked in this idiom ever since.

The task of creating the pictures and my relationship with the image has a twofold reality – 'It takes its course as human existence and, at the

'The Celtic Awakening' (1987) ▶

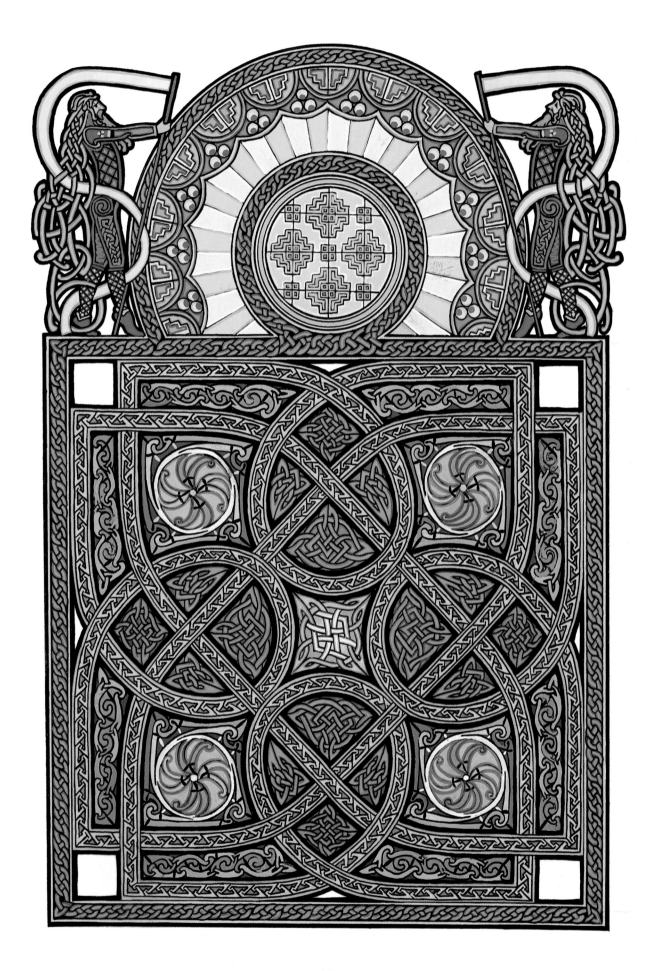

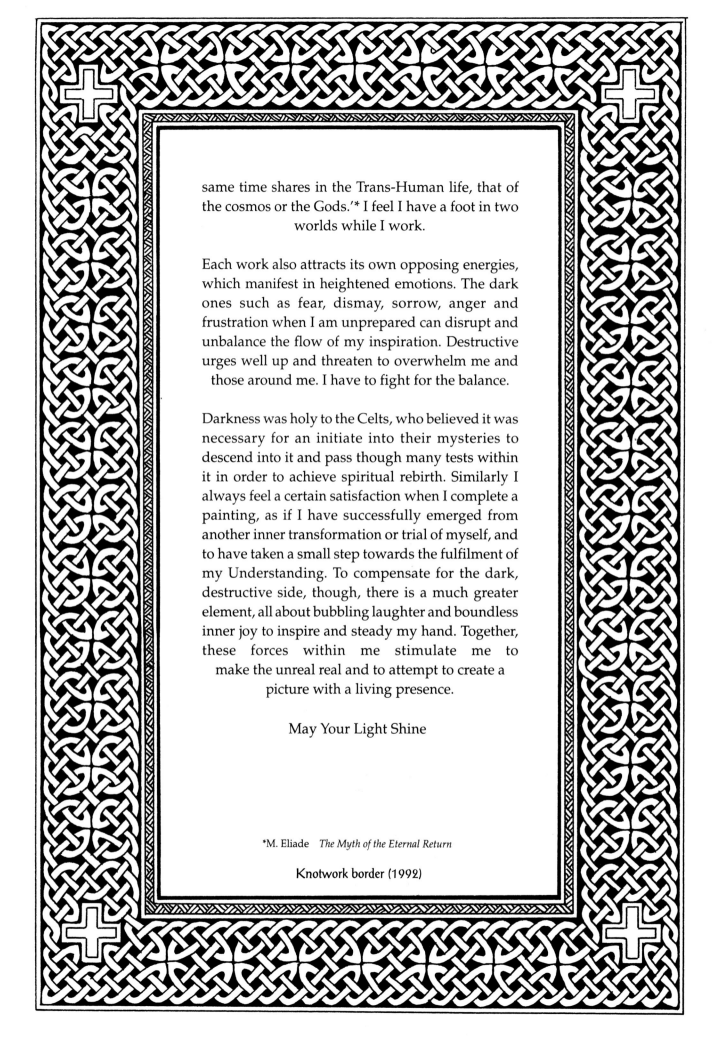

same time shares in the Trans-Human life, that of the cosmos or the Gods.'* I feel I have a foot in two worlds while I work.

Each work also attracts its own opposing energies, which manifest in heightened emotions. The dark ones such as fear, dismay, sorrow, anger and frustration when I am unprepared can disrupt and unbalance the flow of my inspiration. Destructive urges well up and threaten to overwhelm me and those around me. I have to fight for the balance.

Darkness was holy to the Celts, who believed it was necessary for an initiate into their mysteries to descend into it and pass though many tests within it in order to achieve spiritual rebirth. Similarly I always feel a certain satisfaction when I complete a painting, as if I have successfully emerged from another inner transformation or trial of myself, and to have taken a small step towards the fulfilment of my Understanding. To compensate for the dark, destructive side, though, there is a much greater element, all about bubbling laughter and boundless inner joy to inspire and steady my hand. Together, these forces within me stimulate me to make the unreal real and to attempt to create a picture with a living presence.

May Your Light Shine

*M. Eliade *The Myth of the Eternal Return*

Knotwork border (1992)

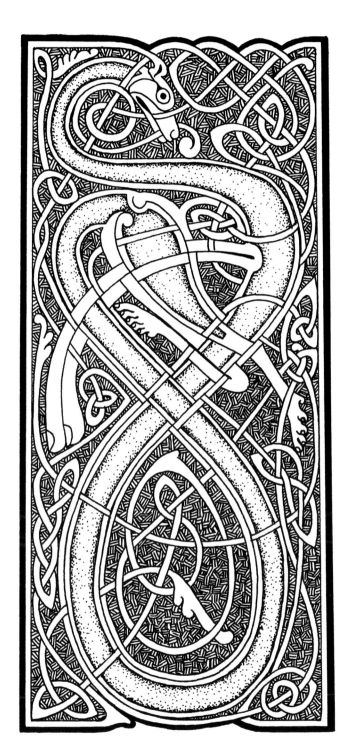

'The Celtic Dog' (1992)

REBIRTH

FROM THE 5000-year history of the Celtic peoples, whose ancestors once inhabited Europe and whose posterity persists everywhere, Celtic art contains the only expression of the suppressd Western mystery tradition still alive today. It has undergone many transformations and revivals, but is still intuitively genuine and shines down the centuries like a beacon. Courtney Davis's acclaimed work is a contemporary statement of those newly ancient sacred mysteries and their symbols. The conventions and style he uses are absolutely authentic and are themselves the result of over ten years' patient learning of the lost, detailed crafts required before inspiration can transform colour and symbolism into the fine art of these truly magical paintings.

From pagan, druidic roots, the unbroken thread was woven into the fabric of Gnostic Christianity (the term for initiation into individual enlightenment beyond words and dogma), into the Grail legends, on into the Lindisfarne Gospels and the Book of Kells, and beyond that, carrying on the immortal power of the human spirit itself into the 20th century – now.

The light passed, as it always had, through the arts and crafts of its custodians, artists in every field, sometimes a dormant seed, sometimes flowering in obscure places where the sacred waters of life remained. Wherever and whenever it happened, it echoed in the inherited dormant race memory of Western man, waiting like the archetypal Arthur for the call to awareness of destiny and identity in time of greatest need.

The Celts knew, because they experienced it as a fact through initiation into their mysteries, that they (and by implication all men whether they knew it or not) were spiritually immortal. Their magic lay in *knowing* that death and rebirth were facts of experience, not of *belief.* They were in consequence fearless individualists in war and lived life exuberantly and with vigour. They had a great opinion of themselves, these heroes of deathless legend.

The blaze of psychic energy generated by these certainties – 'The Bright Knowledge' – has survived political dominion and religious persecution, both systematic assaults on the integrity of the individual, channelled in art along the sacred thread that binds the present to the past, and the universe itself together.

The 'decorative' quality in true Celtic art is directly related to the perception of a sacro-magical pattern of cosmic energy in nature, the emotional or felt equivalent of the modern chaos theory, expressed artistically rather than scientifically, adding the human dimension of feeling to perceptions of reality. The result was magic. The coinage of perception was minted on both sides: good value.

In fact, they are not 'decorations' at all, but precise and symbolic statements of a vision of reality. That reality included other universes, 'otherworlds' in some sense existing alongside ours, displaced from us sideways in time. It is strangely similar to the more recent speculations of the new physics.

When the balance of energies was right, all went well, but when the pattern was disturbed, ills arose.

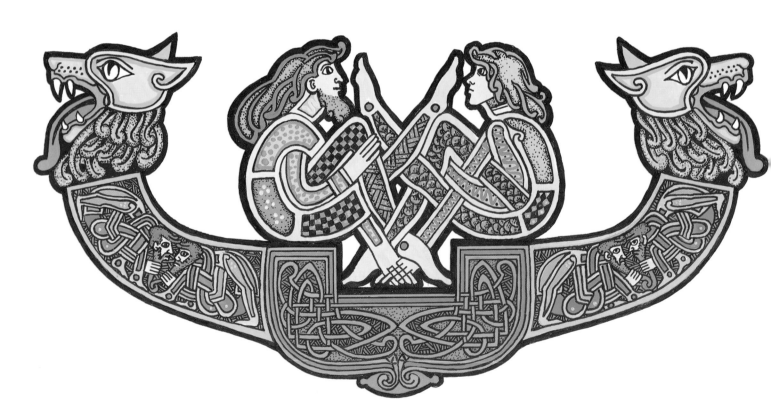

'Friendship' (1992)

'The Consecration of Awareness' (1992) ▶

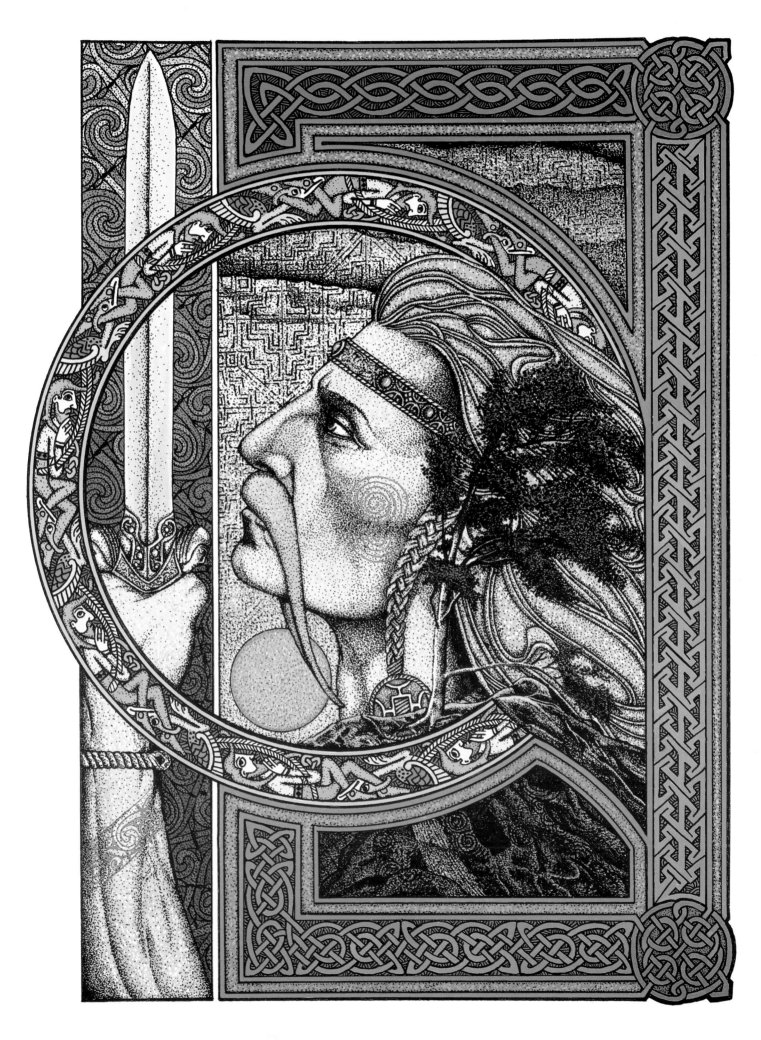

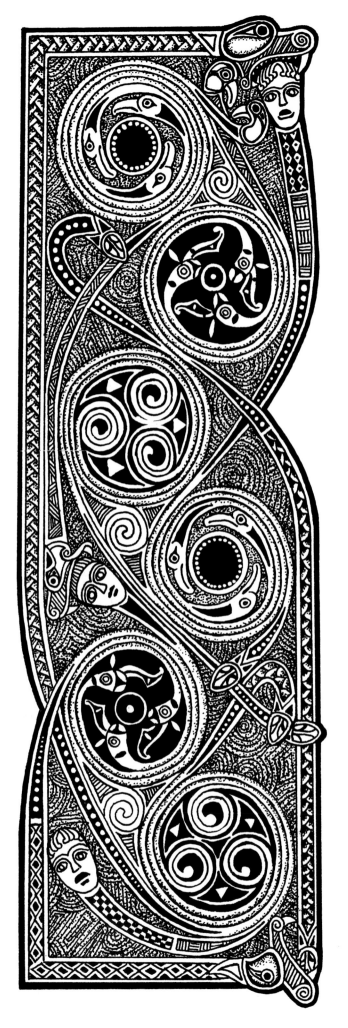

This perception was derived directly from nature, and extended to the inner spiritual and psychic realities of mankind. This was not pantheism at all, but a sophisticated and accurate analysis as true then as it is today. Man, out of balance with his own nature, created an empty wasteland in and around himself – and called it order.

The detailed decorative frameworks that form an integral part of Courtney Davis's images contain the traditional symbols of the Celts' transcendental vision of nature, the cosmos and the human soul. Symbols – that is, visual or verbal metaphor (parable and myth) – are the only known way of expressing the so-called 'mystical' transcendental union of inner opposites essential to the psychic wholeness – the irrational and the rational. Individual and collective madness resulting in self-destruction arise from a self split away from its true nature, or 'dissociated' in the jargon of psychology.

Just as light itself cannot be comprehended by the science of nuclear physics unless simultaneously as a particle and a wave, and in mathematically precise symbols at that, so sacred symbols are the universal language of the inner cosmos, the inscapes of the human psyche. Its constants are just as capable of being irrational numbers. They are in fact the archetypes of the collective subconscious mind identified only in this century by the psychiatrist C. G. Jung, and illustrated as they were and are manifest in our own genetic and cultural identity, rather than that of the East. In this book they will strike unmistakable chords within you. Do not be afraid of their fascination. They are old, heady wine in a new cup.

These ancient intuitive perceptions, preserved down the centuries, show how wrong it is to assume that the most significant achievements of the human spirit are also the most recent, or that the wheel never has to be reinvented. They suggest that the intangible and unquantifiable side of the human psyche has been crowded out by emphasis

Adaptation of part of 8th century gilt bronze mount (1992)

on mere reason, leaving an emptiness and lack of identity in the heart of modern man.

Any challenge to reason has always been felt as a challenge to authority, whose priorities are different, and suppressed with vigour. That was the political fate of the Celts. Spiritually, the Celtic vision has survived. 'It is our turn now, and the call is to the Celt' – a line from Hugh MacDiarmid – is not about St George's struggle with temporal evil, but about St Michael's final battle with spiritual evil. It is fundamental. The whole *is* greater than the sum of its parts. That is the mystery of life. Two and two can make five; humour, honesty, courage and inspiration cannot be measured, and love is not rational, but it does make the world go round.

It is time to restore the balance. Courtney's work retrieves in a visual way some lost ancestral knowledge and understanding of the Western tradition, and shows the reality of the point of balance between the two worlds we all must inhabit to restore ourselves and the natural world that is our origin and our home.

It is blindingly simple: we must change. First, we must learn to love and heal our alienated selves, as the precondition for loving our fellow men, by retrieving what has been taken from us. Only then can we love the other, outer manifestations of God, the Earth, the universe and the mysterious unity of all created things evident to those with eyes to see. The Celtic vision goes out.

It has been a privilege to support Courtney Davis financially and with my faith while he was making this book. I wish that I had been able to bear some of his pain.

CHRIS ROBERTS

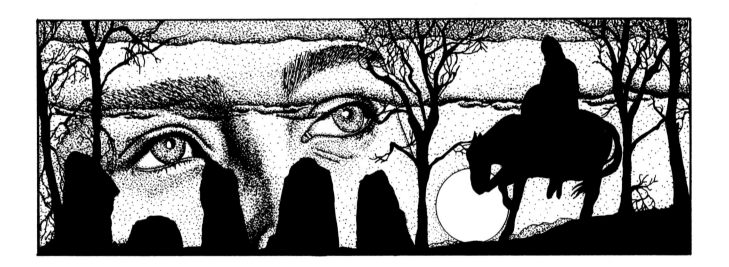

A sense of something far more deeply interfused,
Whose dwelling is the light of setting suns.

WILLIAM WORDSWORTH

'The Returning Warrior' (1992)

Time

Take no oath by the earth that you stand on
You walk on it only for a while, but soon
you shall be buried within it.

Pay no heed to the world you live in. You are
dazzled by its pomp and pleasure, but soon
you shall be carried from it.

Time is like the ebbing tide on the beach. You
cannot see it move by staring at it, but soon
it has run away from sight.

From *Celtic Fire*

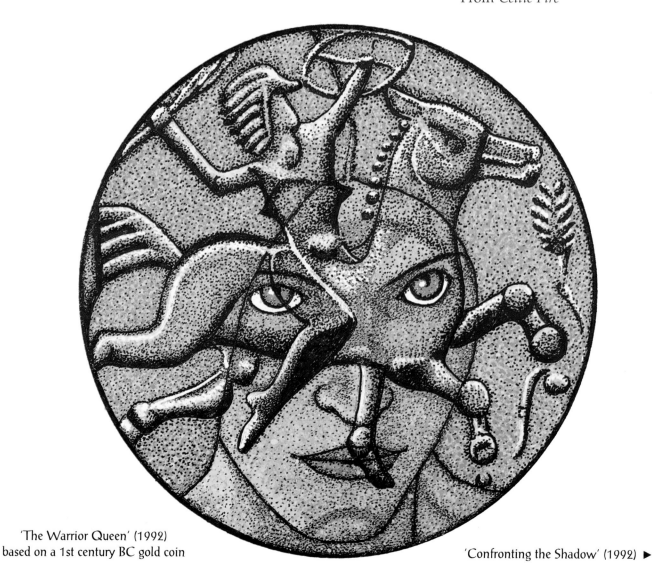

'The Warrior Queen' (1992)
based on a 1st century BC gold coin

'Confronting the Shadow' (1992) ▶

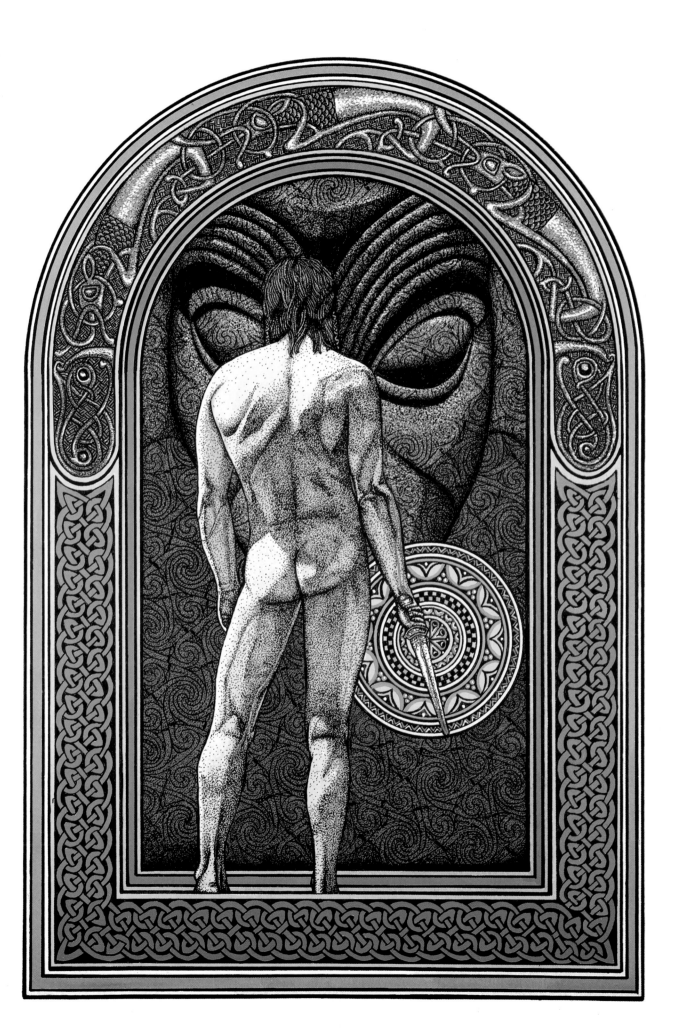

THE OTHERWORLD

To be a fearless warrior among warriors was the ideal of life to a Celt. With their strong love of fighting, to die in battle surrounded by friends and dead enemies was considered a worthy end. But there was much more to it than that. To the Celts the universe was a vast illusion, and they believed themselves to be immortal. Consequently they tended to regard life – which they believed to be predestined – as a game to be played, and had an easy attitude to death. They had a natural acceptance of being able to pass from the physical world to the otherworld with ease, since at most times there was no barrier between the two, but a fine overlapping of the two worlds – dawn or twilight, a sea mist, or a river's edge or bridge.

Making the return journey to the land of mortals was more difficult, and almost impossible for those who had visited the dwelling place of the dead in the otherworld.

The otherworld of the Celts was a place of supreme happiness, rich in food and the delights of nature, a place where no unpleasantness existed. It inspired the poets who yearned for a golden age to tell of the accomplishments of heroes and gods who travelled between the worlds like Tir nan Og, where time ceased to exist, and the physical world. All who inhabited these magical places were immortal, and warriors killed in battle were healed in three days, ready to return to life once more.

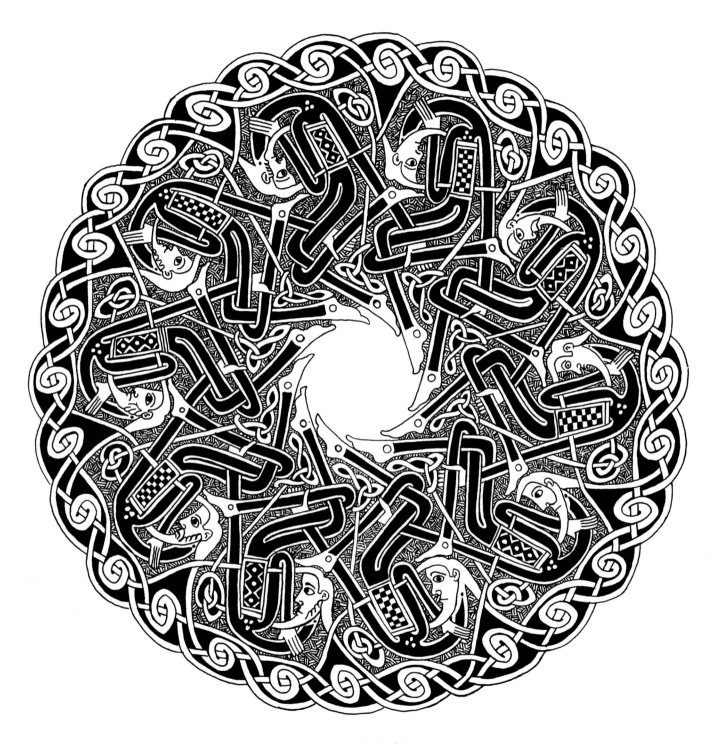

'The Cycle of Rebirth' (1992)

◄ Celtic knotwork border (1992)

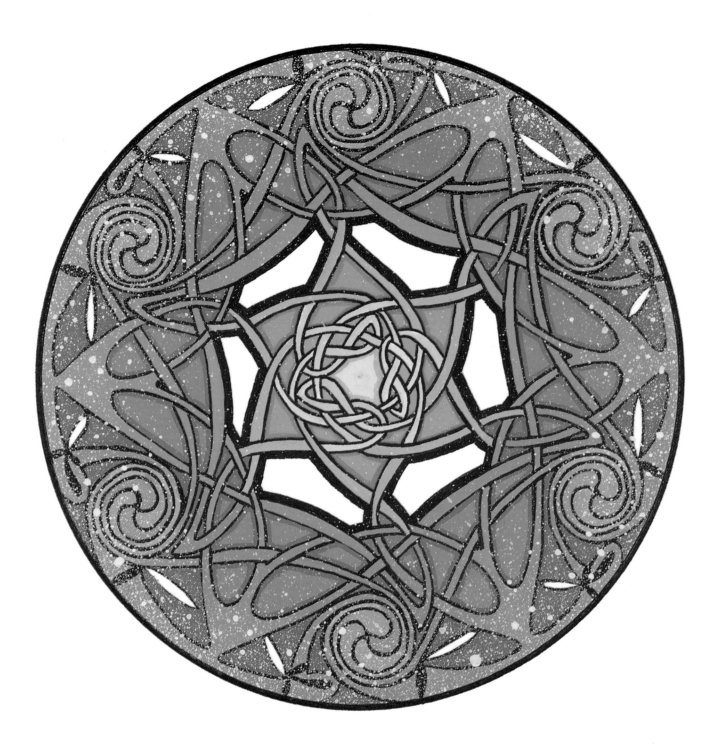

I have been in many shapes before I attained a
congenial form.

'Taliesin's Journey of Experience' (1992)

'The Return from the Otherworld' (1992) ▶

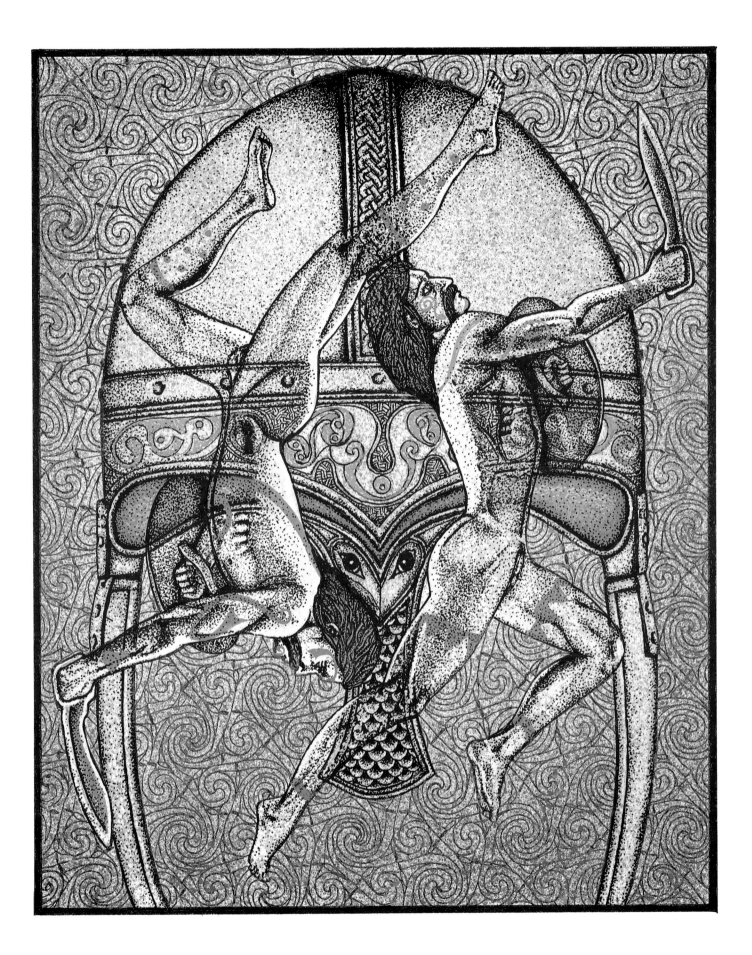

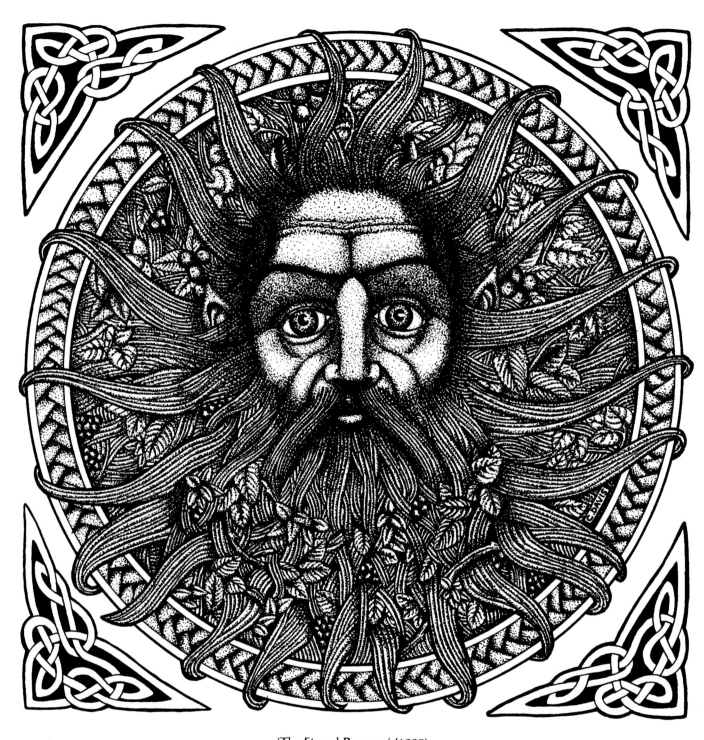

'The Eternal Presence' (1993)

SEAT OF
THE SOUL

THE CELTS believed the head to be supremely powerful, so to leave the head of a dead warrior lying after battle was to degrade its power. It was believed to be both the sacred and human centre and the resting place of the soul. The Celtic warriors preserved their trophies in cedar oil, for they believed that the potency of the head remained and that the power within the dead warrior could now be used by its possessor. Hung from his horse or nailed to the doorway of his house, it would guard him from evil.

The heads were also closely connected to water worship. Many have been discovered at holy wells and pools which were sacred power sources to the Celts; ceremonies there included the use of skulls as drinking vessels.

'Seat of the Soul' (1992)

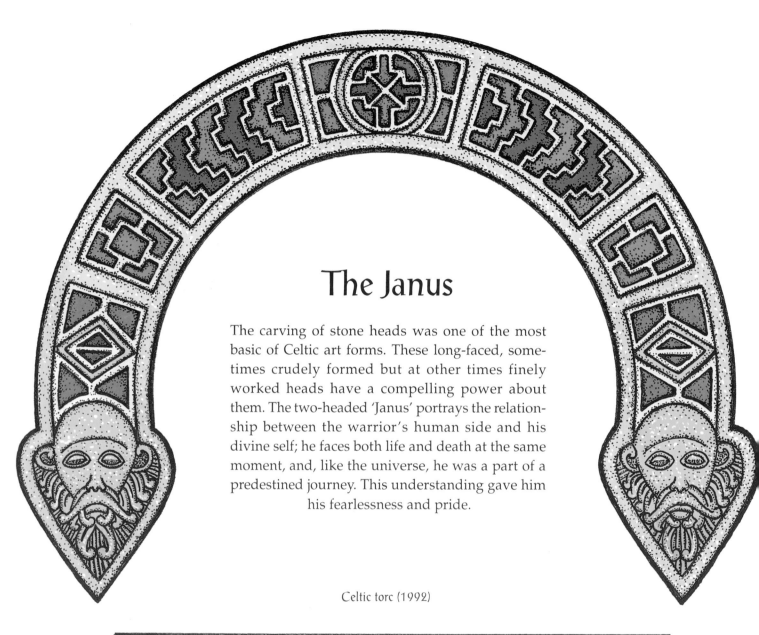

The Janus

The carving of stone heads was one of the most basic of Celtic art forms. These long-faced, sometimes crudely formed but at other times finely worked heads have a compelling power about them. The two-headed 'Janus' portrays the relationship between the warrior's human side and his divine self; he faces both life and death at the same moment, and, like the universe, he was a part of a predestined journey. This understanding gave him his fearlessness and pride.

Celtic torc (1992)

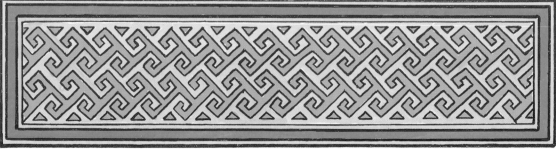

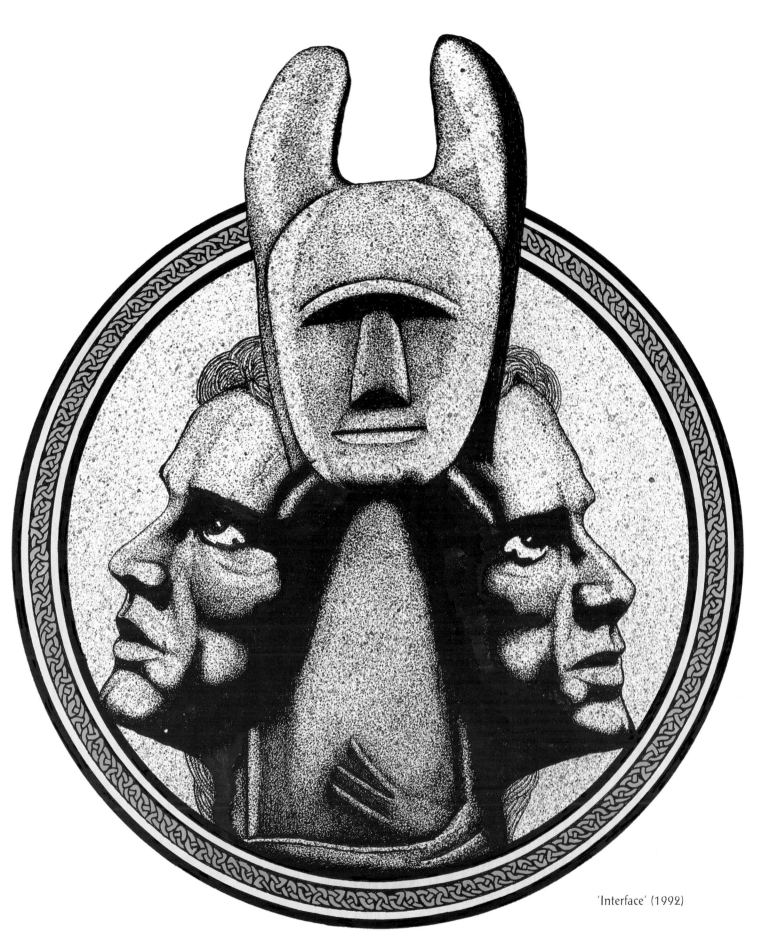

'Interface' (1992)

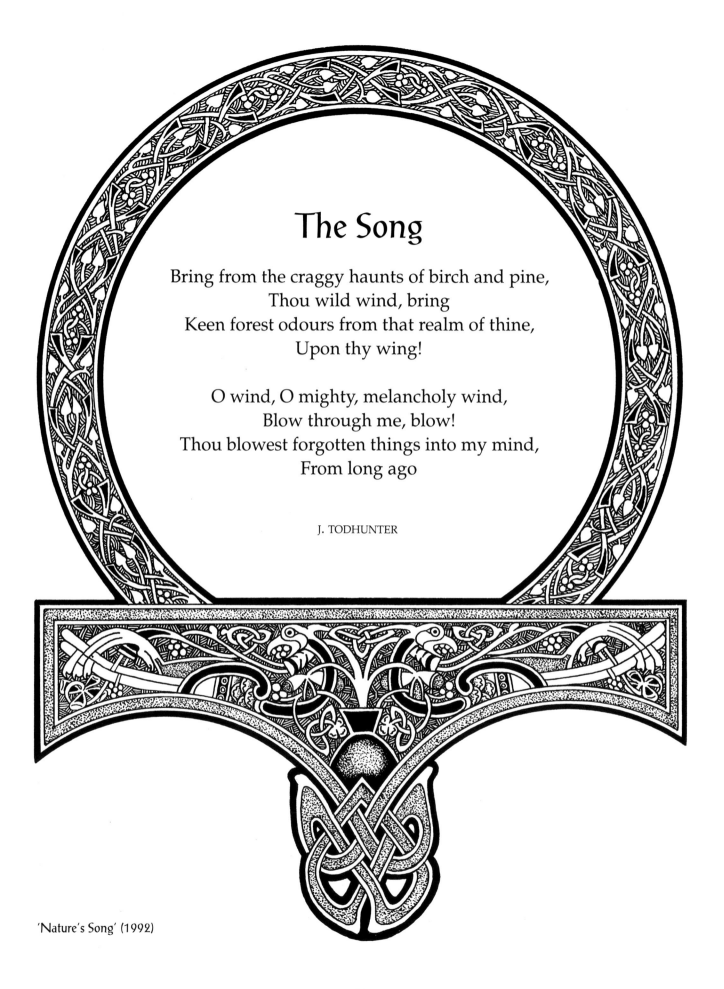

The Song

Bring from the craggy haunts of birch and pine,
Thou wild wind, bring
Keen forest odours from that realm of thine,
Upon thy wing!

O wind, O mighty, melancholy wind,
Blow through me, blow!
Thou blowest forgotten things into my mind,
From long ago

J. TODHUNTER

'Nature's Song' (1992)

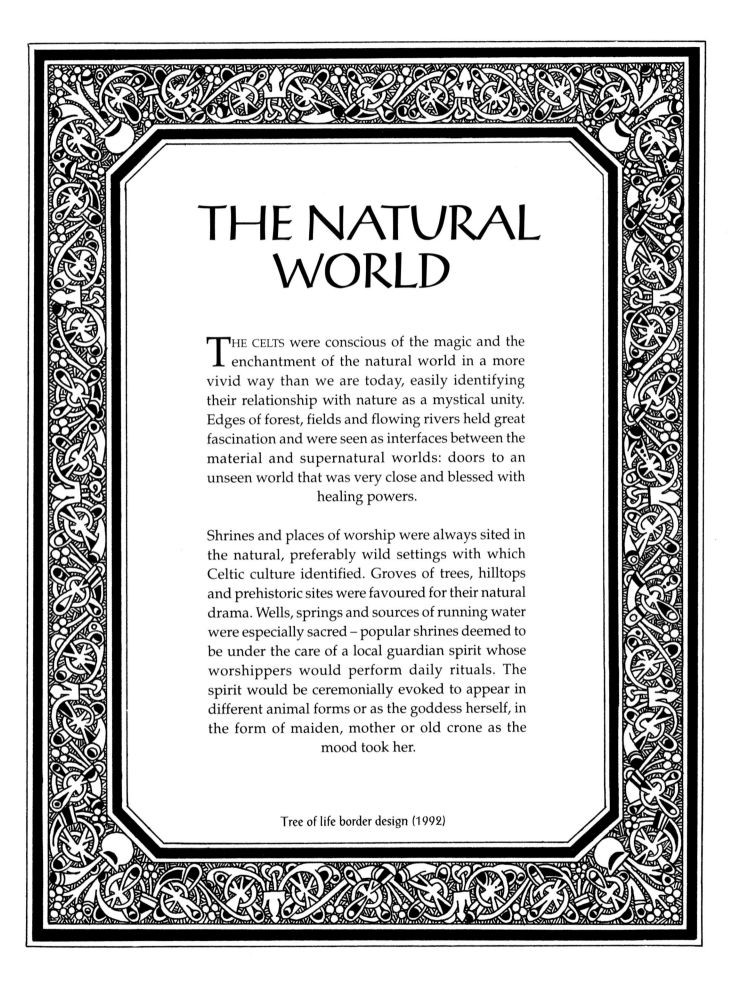

THE NATURAL WORLD

THE CELTS were conscious of the magic and the enchantment of the natural world in a more vivid way than we are today, easily identifying their relationship with nature as a mystical unity. Edges of forest, fields and flowing rivers held great fascination and were seen as interfaces between the material and supernatural worlds: doors to an unseen world that was very close and blessed with healing powers.

Shrines and places of worship were always sited in the natural, preferably wild settings with which Celtic culture identified. Groves of trees, hilltops and prehistoric sites were favoured for their natural drama. Wells, springs and sources of running water were especially sacred – popular shrines deemed to be under the care of a local guardian spirit whose worshippers would perform daily rituals. The spirit would be ceremonially evoked to appear in different animal forms or as the goddess herself, in the form of maiden, mother or old crone as the mood took her.

Tree of life border design (1992)

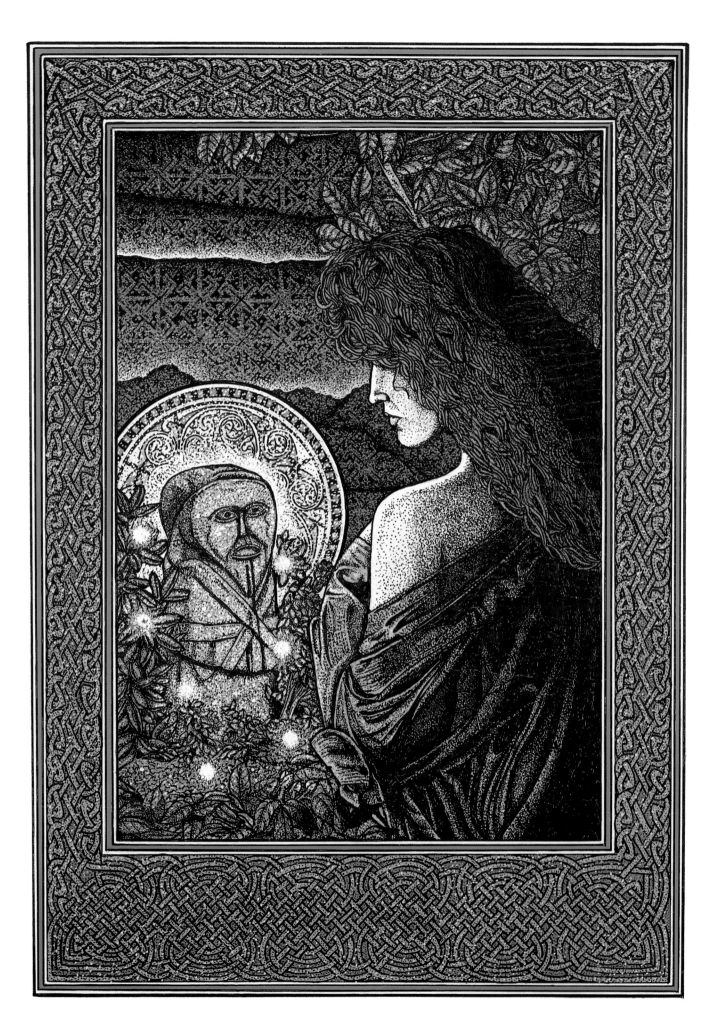

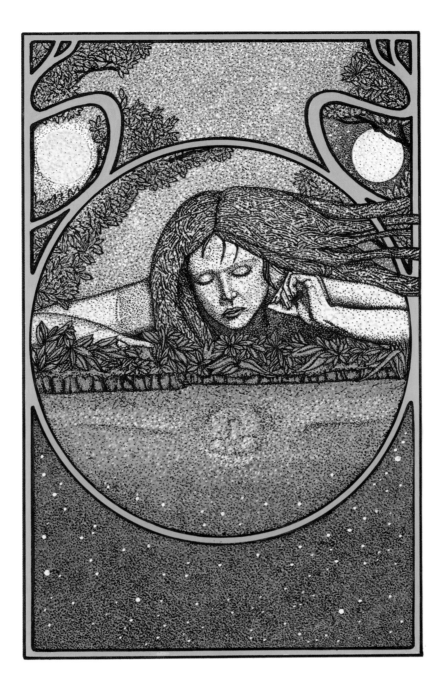

Sacred Water

Water was a major focal point of Celtic spiritual life. From the dawn of man many wells, springs and rivers have been sacred, and some survive hidden away in the depths of the countryside even today. Despite many outward changes in appearance, they are still able to evoke feelings of veneration to the threefold Mother Goddess who protected the sacred site.

'The Dreaming Pool' (1990)

◀ 'The Janus, a Magical Encounter' (1988)

However, water in general was highly sacred and significant, and in fact the largest finds of Celtic artefacts have been found in lakes and rivers, where they seem to have been thrown as votive offerings. Water with specific therapeutic properties was especially venerated, in cults centred on particular wells so powerful that they were later specifically Christianized to rid them of their centuries of pagan association.

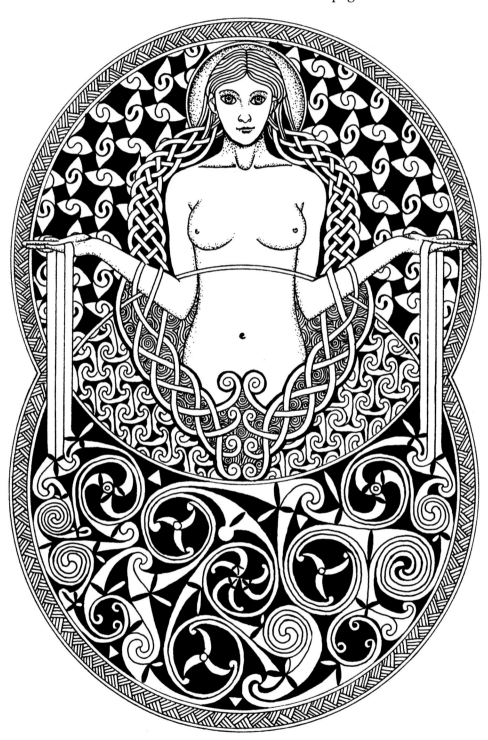

'Guardian of the Well' (1992)

TOTEM ANIMALS

Broadly speaking, every Celtic sacred animal represented certain energies or forces active in the material world, and had a corresponding god or godess as the expression of those forces on a cosmic level. There was thus a relationship between the primal energy and the governing deity, corresponding to the Celtic vision of the three worlds. Reality itself was an expression of an overlap, so that to every manifested thing in nature could be attributed characteristics of each sphere in addition to its mere appearance in the Earth world.

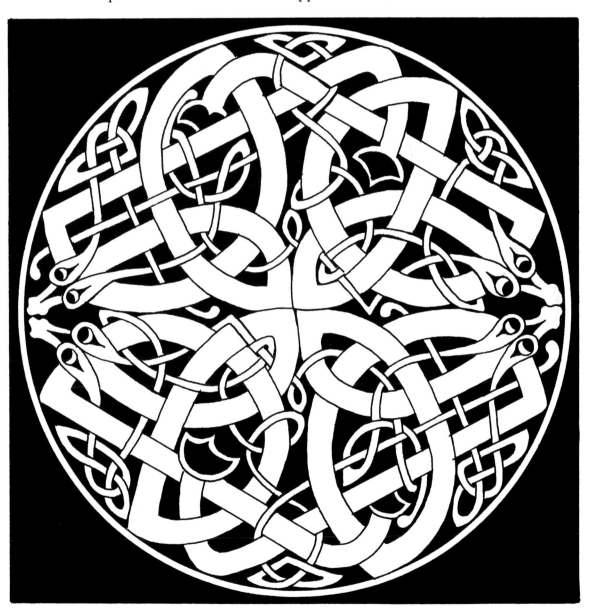

'Entwined Serpents' (1992)

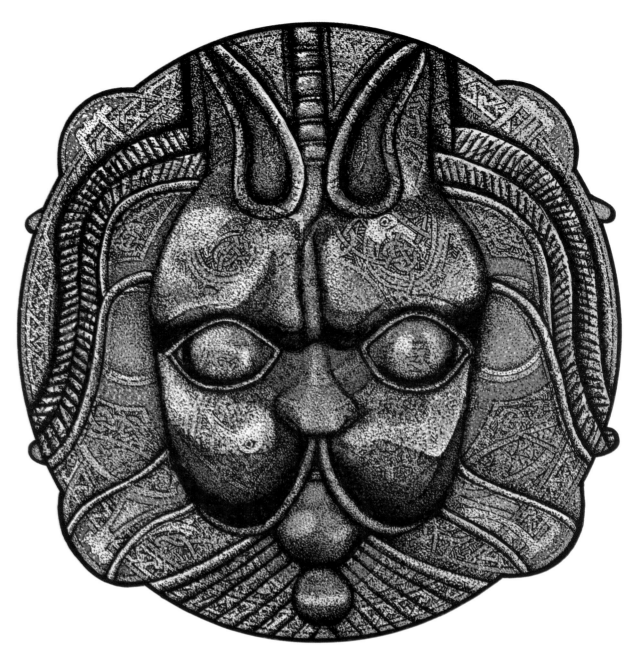

'Pagan Echo' (1992)

Animals embodied the energies of the land, or Earth world, and the underworld, but the associated divinity was the higher link to the spiritual sphere. The energies of certain animals were adopted by tribes or individuals as totems to bring good luck in the form of manifested characteristics such as ferocity, speed or the ability to inspire fear.

The names of the gods in fables and myths designed to illustrate the concept varied from place to place; for example, Irish myths are different from Welsh and French ones in the stories told, though the underlying concepts are strikingly consistent as they are in all mythology. Celtic inventiveness and imagination while telling stories featuring particular characters or heroes could result in misleading details being added for dramatic effect. The key lies in recognizing the underlying symbolism.

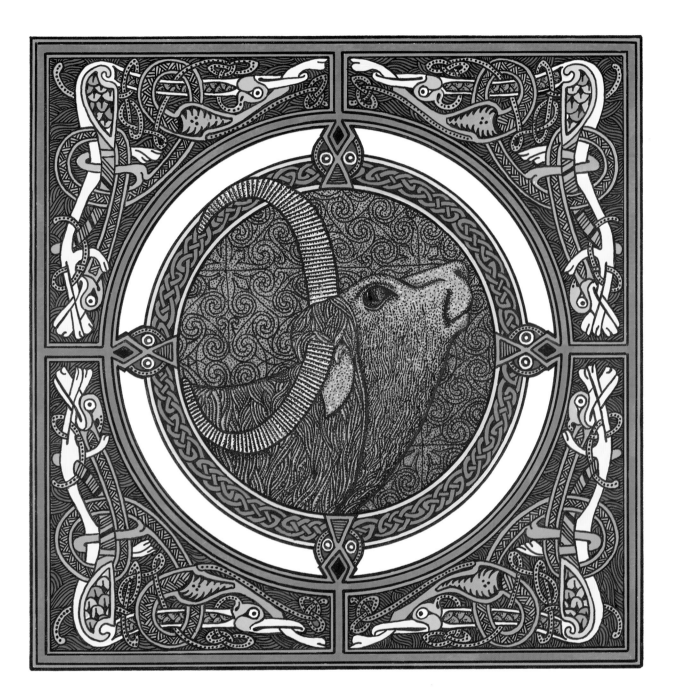

The Bull

The bull represents primal male energy surmounted by the symbol of the Eternal Feminine in the moon shape of its horns. Its main role seems to have been in ritual sacrifice, and its skin was used by shamans to induce the gifts of seership and prophecy. It is unclear which deity was specifically associated with it – indeed, it might have been an expression of two principles in unity.

'The Mighty Hu' (1992)

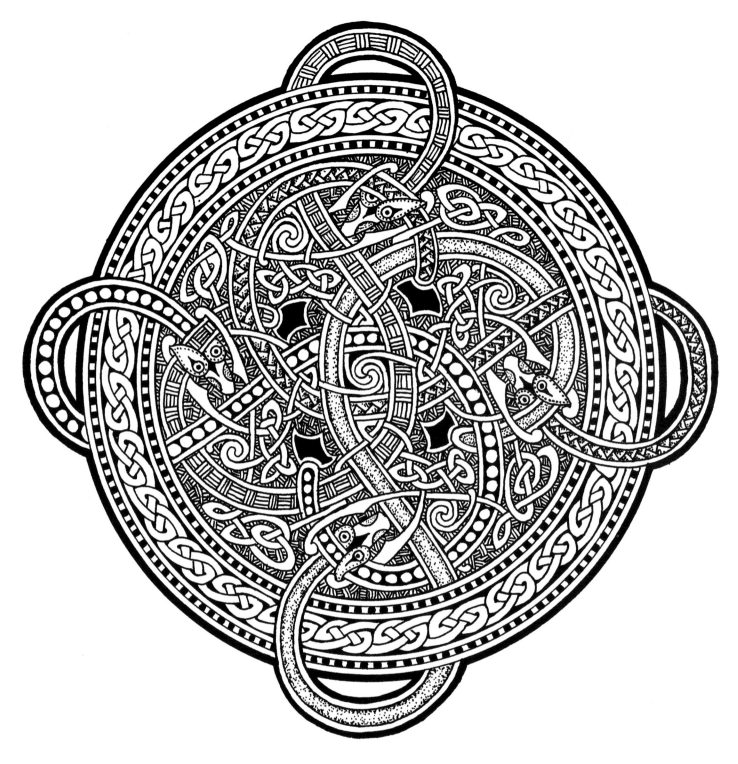

The Serpent

A creature of the underworld, the serpent was considered to be magical because of its knowledge of what happens there concerning the mysteries of death, life and rebirth. It was associated with the lord of the underworld, and was not evil in the modern sense at all.

'The Serpent' (1992)

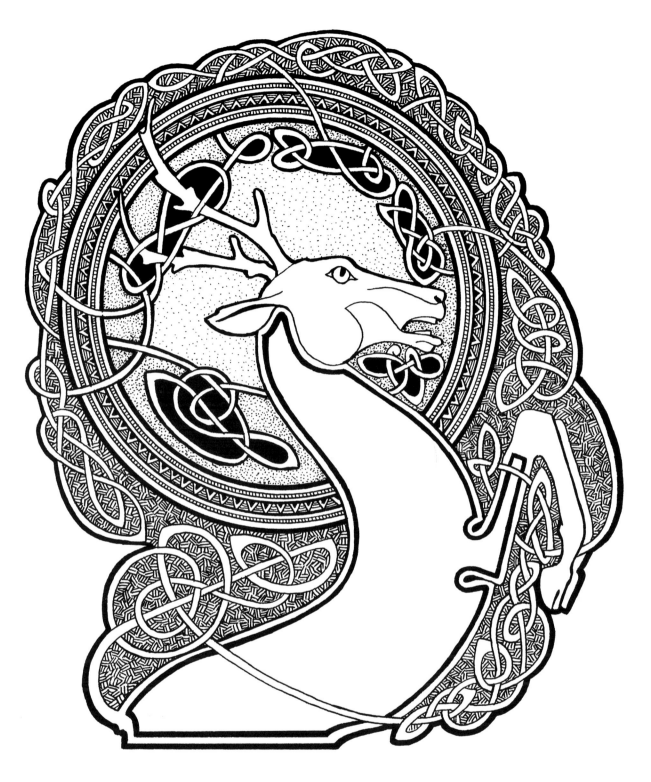

The Stag

The majesty of the stag and its awesome animal presence with antlers for fighting and gaining domination was associated with the lord of the animals – the Horned God. This god was wild and untameable, very much the essence of the male side of nature.

'Lord of All Stags' (1992)

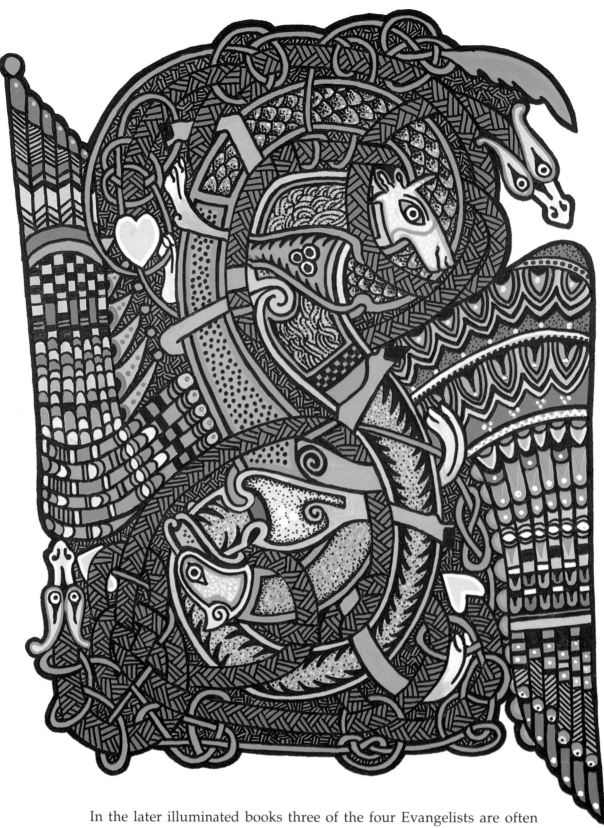

In the later illuminated books three of the four Evangelists are often depicted in animal forms: the lion for Mark, the calf for Luke and the eagle for John.

'Balance' (1992)

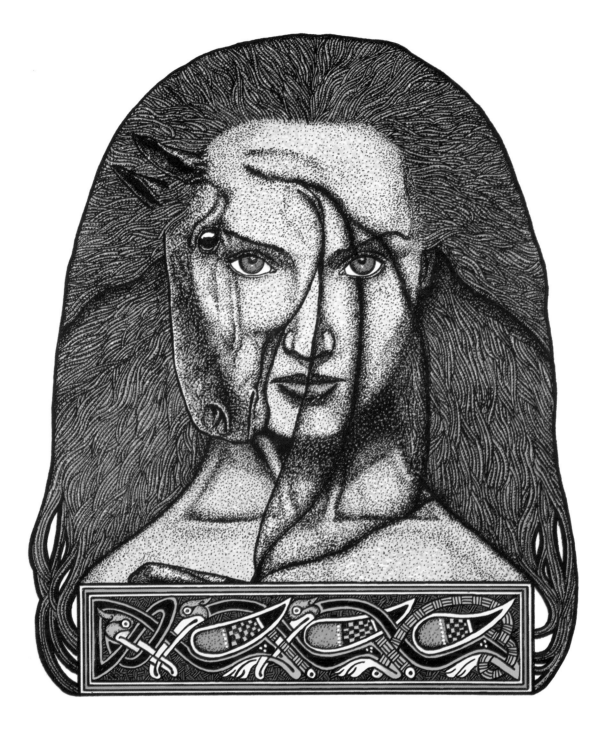

The Horse

Vital to the warrior, strong, swift and beloved of the Celts, the horse spelled exhilaration and a peculiar closeness with the rider. The goddess normally associated with it was probably the Great High Queen herself, who governed the tribal kings and had the aspect of creativity and power.

'Epona' (1992)

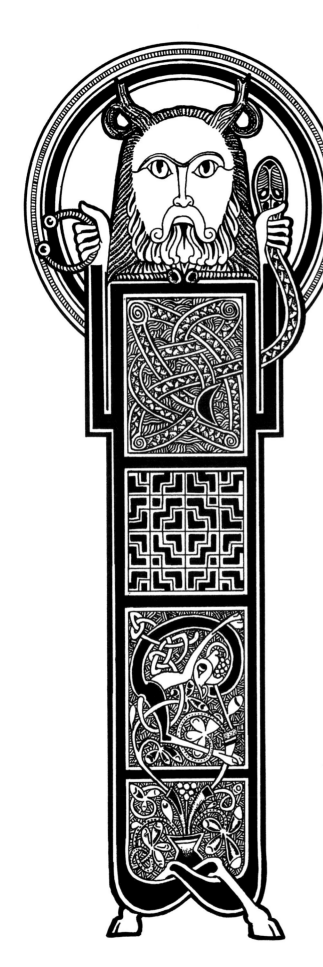

CERNUNNOS, THE HORNED GOD

Fʀᴏᴍ prehistoric times there have been images of horned gods; the earliest image of Cernunnos that has been found dates from around the 4th century BC and comes from northern Italy. Today his name is still preserved in various place names such as Cerne Abbas and in the legend of Herne the Hunter. Though he was banned by St Augustine and the early Church, his image is still active in many rituals and folk dances performed around the countryside.

The most dramatic image of Cernunnos – lord of the animals, plants and water – has him sitting in deep meditation on the side of the Gundestrup Cauldron, his legs folded, holding in one hand a ram's head serpent – the symbol of rebirth – and an emblem of power in the other. Hand outstretched, he offers a torc like the one he himself is wearing, symbolizing the sun and representing the higher self. Around the seated god a number of animals are placed as well as vegetation, illustrating some of the forms of his many manifestations.

'Cernunnos' (1992)

44

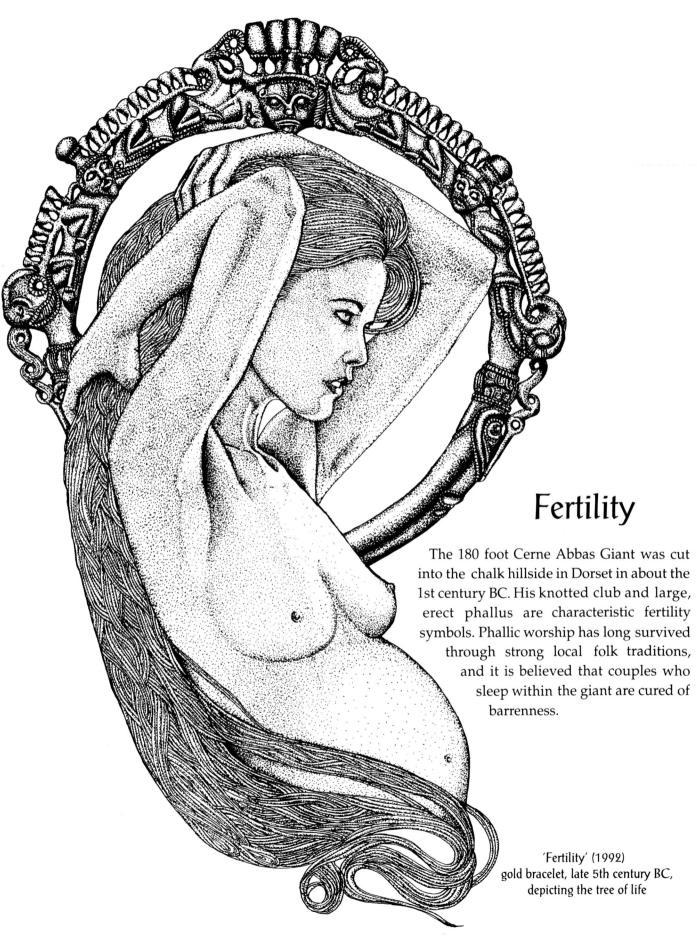

Fertility

The 180 foot Cerne Abbas Giant was cut into the chalk hillside in Dorset in about the 1st century BC. His knotted club and large, erect phallus are characteristic fertility symbols. Phallic worship has long survived through strong local folk traditions, and it is believed that couples who sleep within the giant are cured of barrenness.

'Fertility' (1992)
gold bracelet, late 5th century BC,
depicting the tree of life

45

Lord of the Animals

Cernunnos sits before a silver cauldron, a sacred receptacle prominent in many Celtic legends. Immersion in it altered consciousness from one state to another, similar to the effect of the Christian baptismal font.

In his role as a hunter, animal god and guardian of the gateway to the underworld, Cernunnos controlled the active forces for the giving or taking away of life through selection or sacrifice in nature.

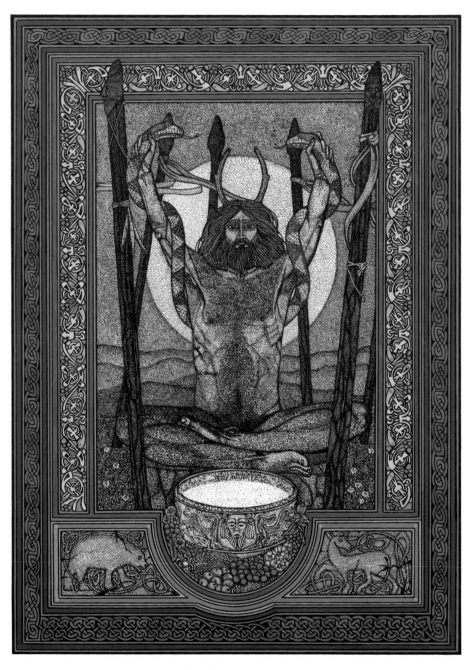

'Lord of the Animals' (1989)
painting for **Celtic Gods, Celtic Goddesses**

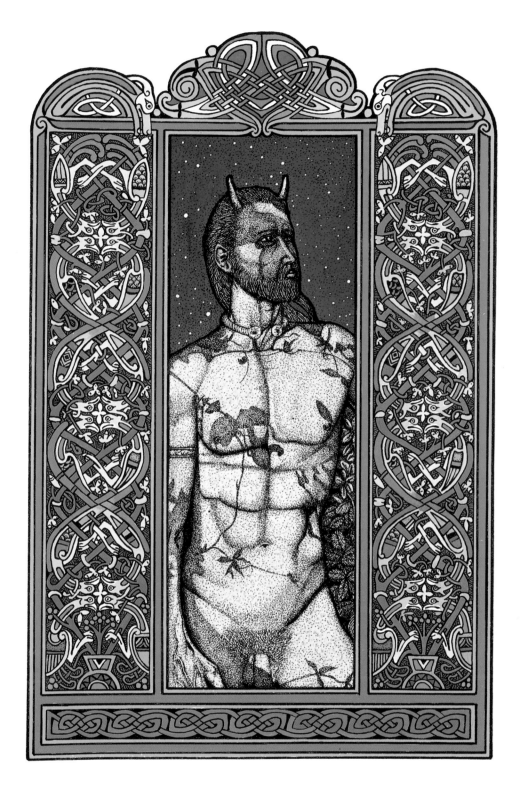

The Cosmic Green Man

As the archetypal spirit of nature, Cernunnos was central to early Celtic
religion. He constantly reappears in Western folklore as the Green Man,
Robin Hood and so on.

'The Cosmic Green Man' (1992)

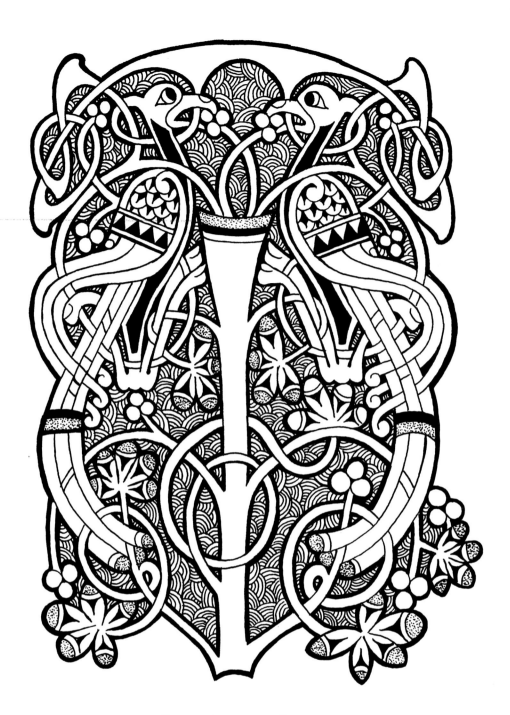

The Sacred Tree

Trees were sacred because their roots lay in the underworld, their trunks in the Earth world, and their branches reached into the sky world. Mistletoe held a special place because it is rooted above the ground in the bark of trees and was therefore not part of the underworld.

The two birds represent the universal and individualized selves (true self and the ego).

'The Sacred Tree of Life' (1992)

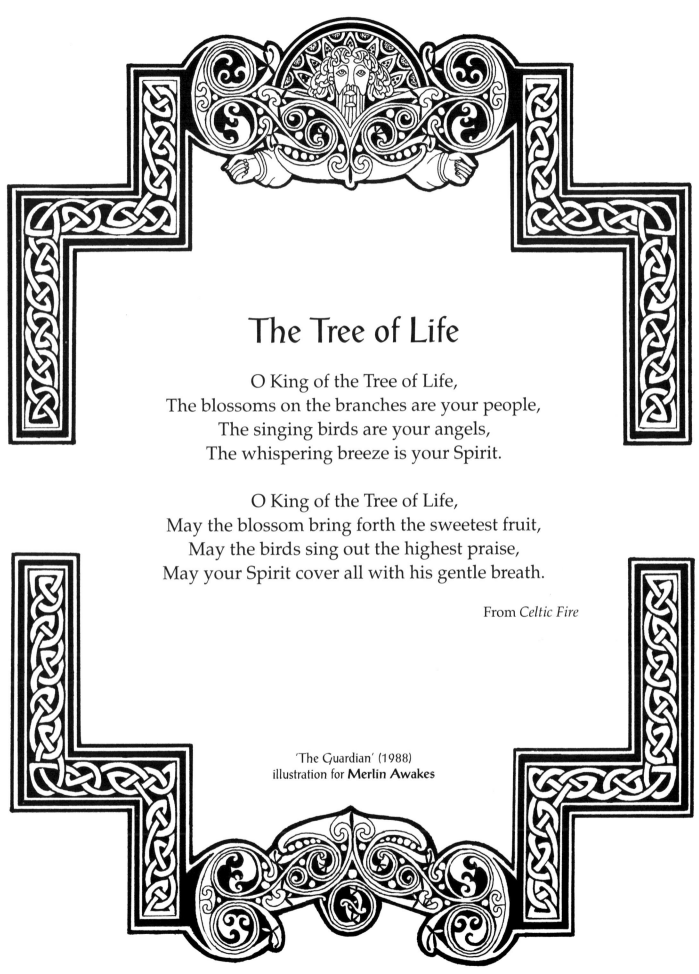

The Tree of Life

O King of the Tree of Life,
The blossoms on the branches are your people,
The singing birds are your angels,
The whispering breeze is your Spirit.

O King of the Tree of Life,
May the blossom bring forth the sweetest fruit,
May the birds sing out the highest praise,
May your Spirit cover all with his gentle breath.

From *Celtic Fire*

'The Guardian' (1988)
illustration for **Merlin Awakes**

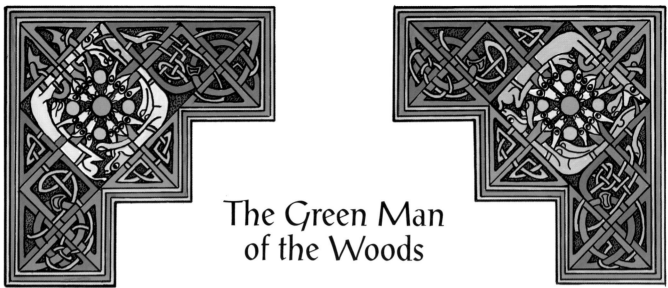

The Green Man
of the Woods

The Green Man embodies the green energy of the trees and the creative force of the tree spirits returning to life after the death imposed by winter. Cernunnos is one of the most misunderstood of the old Celtic gods, and, like the classsical Pan, he was later merged into the Christian horned Devil or false god and his worship was suppressed by the Church. Though at times images of Cernunnos were passionately attacked for what he was believed to represent, we find frequent reminders of him carved in churches. The smiling head of Jack in the Green, surround by vegetation with roots and leaves emerging from his mouth, shows that people still need to be in contact with the spirit of nature.

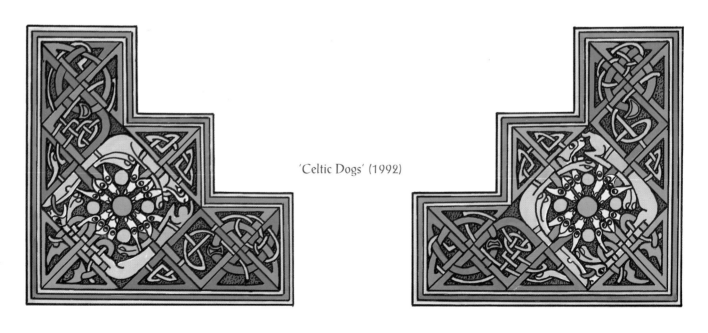

'Celtic Dogs' (1992)

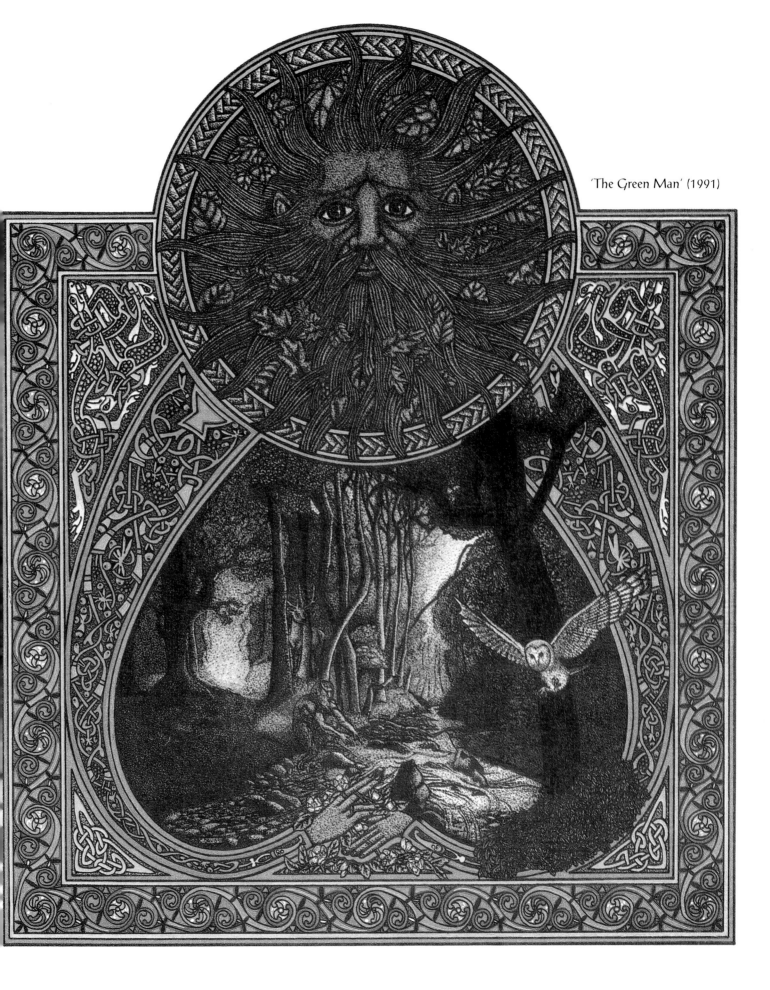

'The Green Man' (1991)

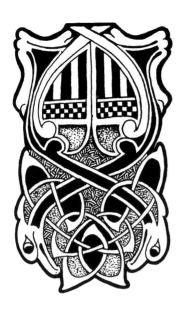

The White Birds

I would that we were, my beloved, white birds on
the foam of the sea!
We tire of the flame of the meteor, before it can pass
by and flee:
And the flame of the blue star of twilight, hung low
on the rim of the sky,
Has wakened in our hearts, my beloved, a sadness
that may never die.

A weariness comes from those dreamers, dew
dabbled, the lily and the rose,
Ah, dream not of them, my beloved, the flame of
the meteor that goes,
Or the flame of the blue star that lingers hung low
in the fall of the dew:
For would we were changed into white birds on the
wandering foam – I and you.

I am haunted by numberless islands, and many a
Danaan shore,
Where Time would surely forget us, and sorrow
come near us no more,
Soon far from the rose and the lily, and the fret of
the flames would we be,
Were we only white birds, my beloved, buoyed out
on the foam of the sea.

W. B. YEATS

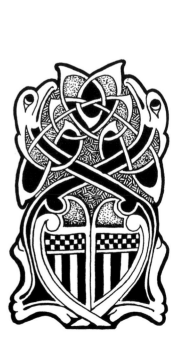

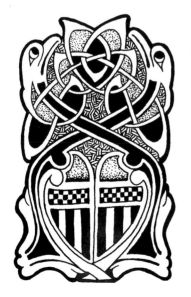

Bird motif (1992)

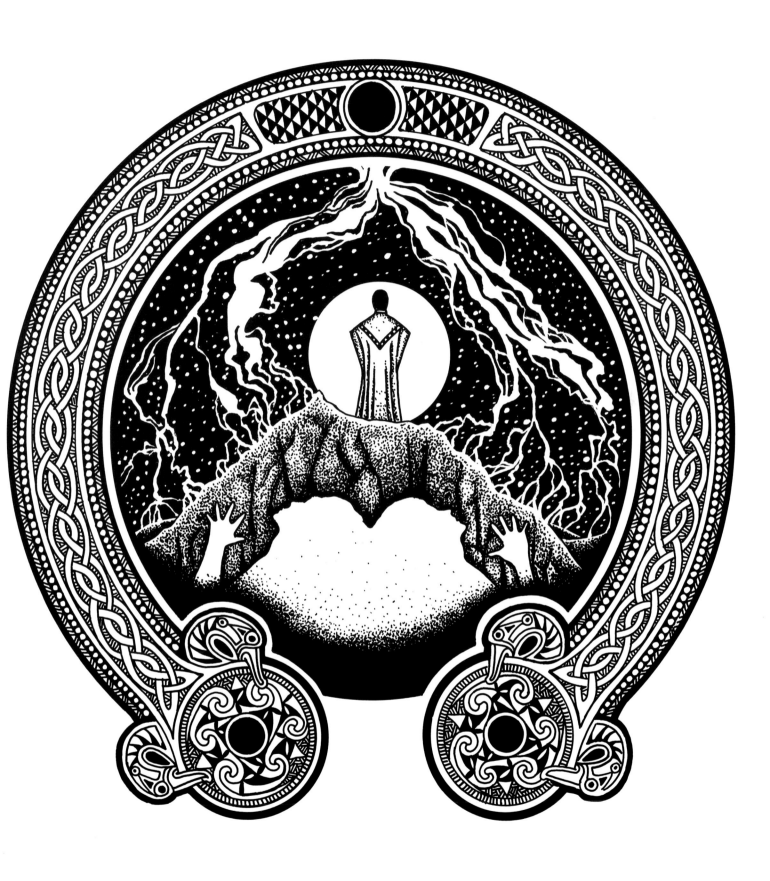

'Sacred Space' (1992)

THE GODDESS
The Mother Goddess

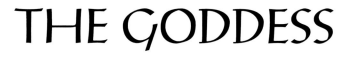

In the past, mankind understood the mystical bonding he had with the Earth. He expressed this with his devotion to the Mother Goddess, who was the Earth and the creator of life and to whom at death he turned. From her, life was formed; mothers, who were guardians of entry to this world, were its completion. The creative magic of the female body became associated with the cyclic pattern of the moon, with its control over water as the visible link with the feminine. The moon was a manifestation of the mother, undergoing, like everything alive, a continual cycle of change. It dies, with but a pause before its regeneration, and is thus a powerful symbol of immortality.

'The Mother' (1992)

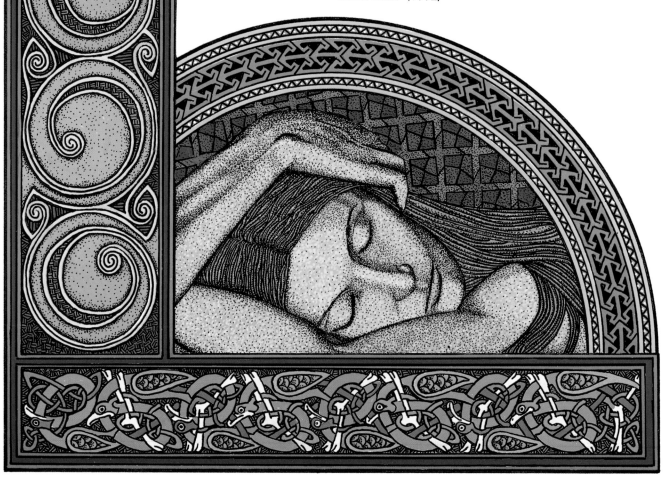

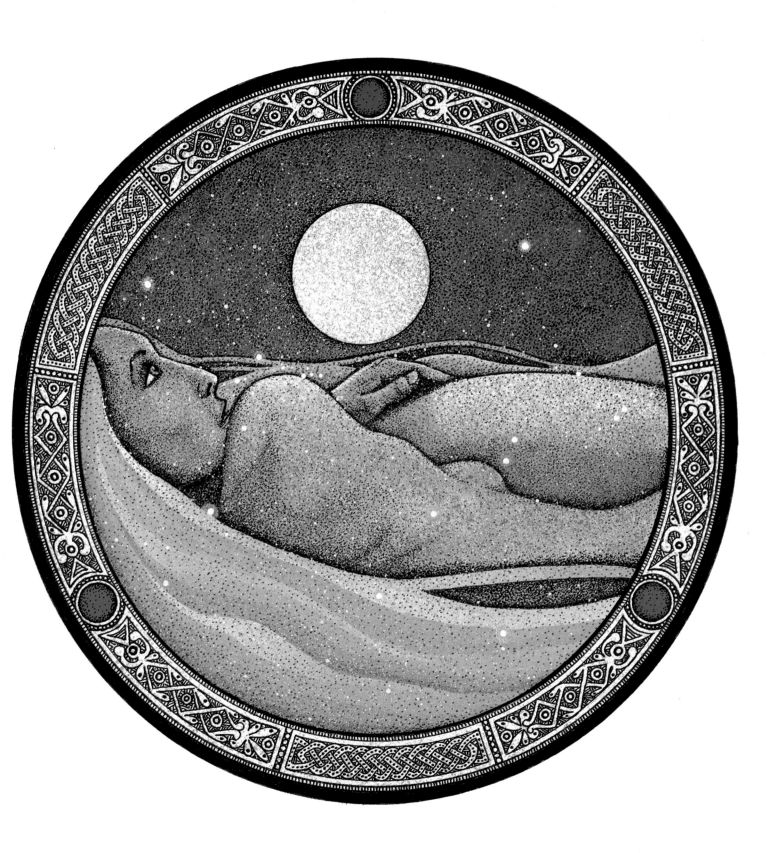

'The Moon Goddess' (1992)

The Great Goddess

The Mother Goddess developed over time, especially in Crete, into belief in the supremacy of the Great Triple Goddess, the eternal feminine. Female saints like St Catherine and St Brighid were venerated by the Celts as Christianized versions of their Great Goddess. This period of belief brought with it many symbols that we know today – among them the ox horns of the fertility moon-earth mother, the labial double axe representing fertility, the serpent, the bird. Unlike the Cretans, however, the Celts accorded equal status to their male and female gods, which was reflected in their status in society. Women, like Boadicea, who successfully took on the might of the Roman legions, could be leaders just as well as men.

The gods of the Irish Celts were the children of the supreme divine mother, the goddess Danu who was also known as Anu or Ana. In Kerry the two mountains called the Paps of Anu are named after her, and are said to represent her breasts and her fertility role. In many Celtic legends women had a greater part to play than their male partners. Legend tells us that whoever wanted to be king of Ireland had first to marry a woman who carried her name, and so the would-be king would mate with the Earth Goddess. There is, however, a darker side to Anu – that of the destroyer. Robert Graves speaks of her as the leader of the Fate Trinity comprising Anu, Badb and Macha. Through destruction, however, change and rebirth can occur.

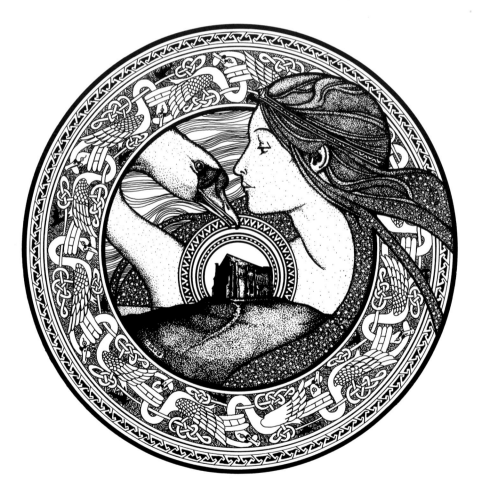

St Catherine's Chapel, Abbotsbury, Dorset (1992)

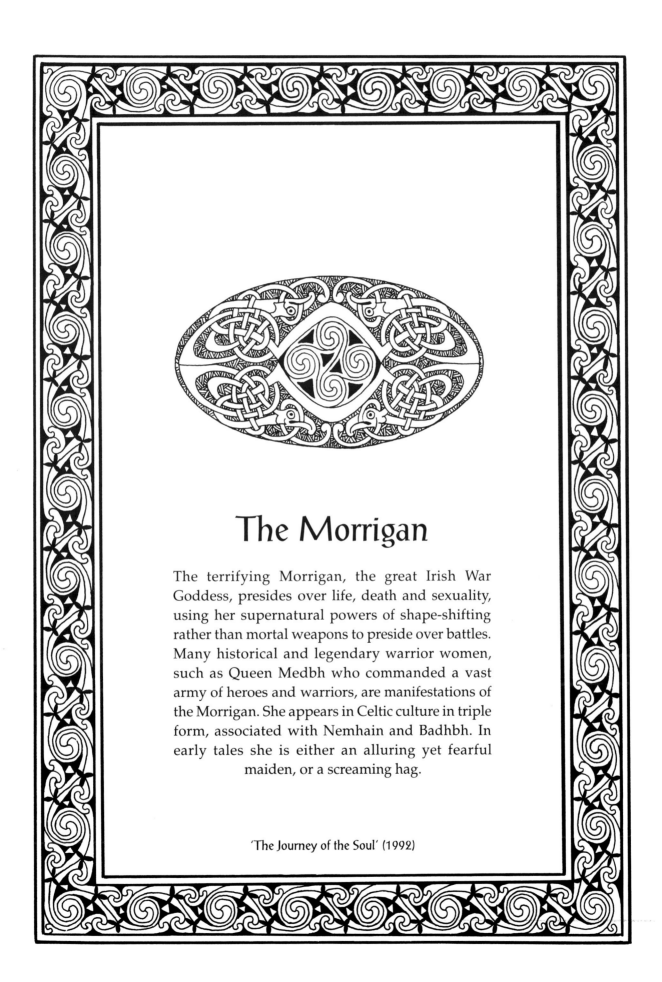

The Morrigan

The terrifying Morrigan, the great Irish War
Goddess, presides over life, death and sexuality,
using her supernatural powers of shape-shifting
rather than mortal weapons to preside over battles.
Many historical and legendary warrior women,
such as Queen Medbh who commanded a vast
army of heroes and warriors, are manifestations of
the Morrigan. She appears in Celtic culture in triple
form, associated with Nemhain and Badhbh. In
early tales she is either an alluring yet fearful
maiden, or a screaming hag.

'The Journey of the Soul' (1992)

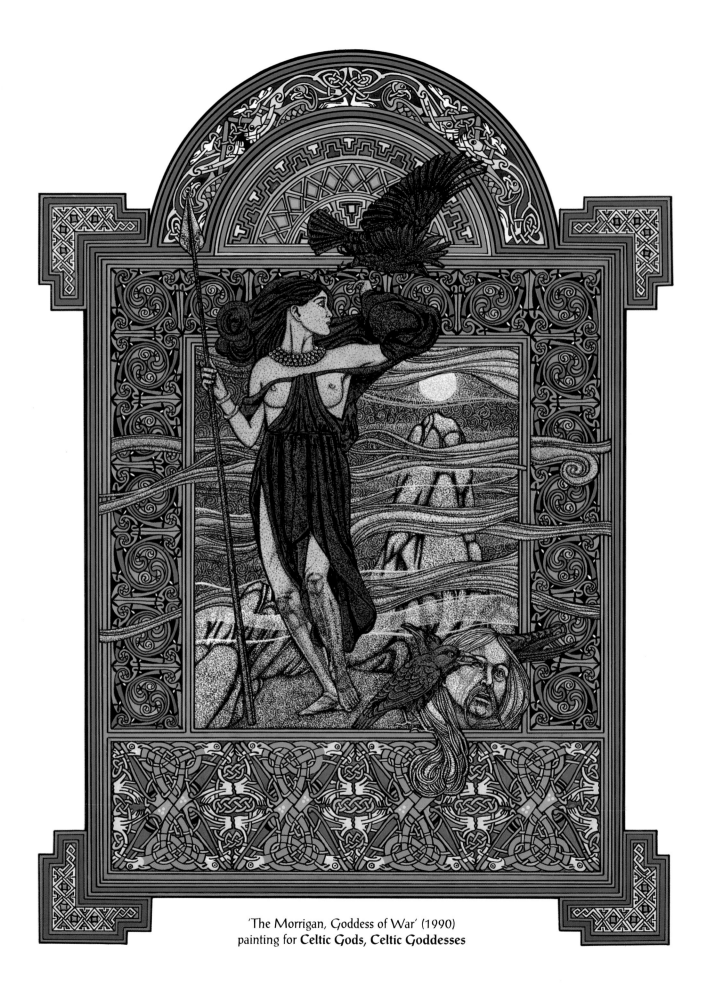

'The Morrigan, Goddess of War' (1990)
painting for **Celtic Gods, Celtic Goddesses**

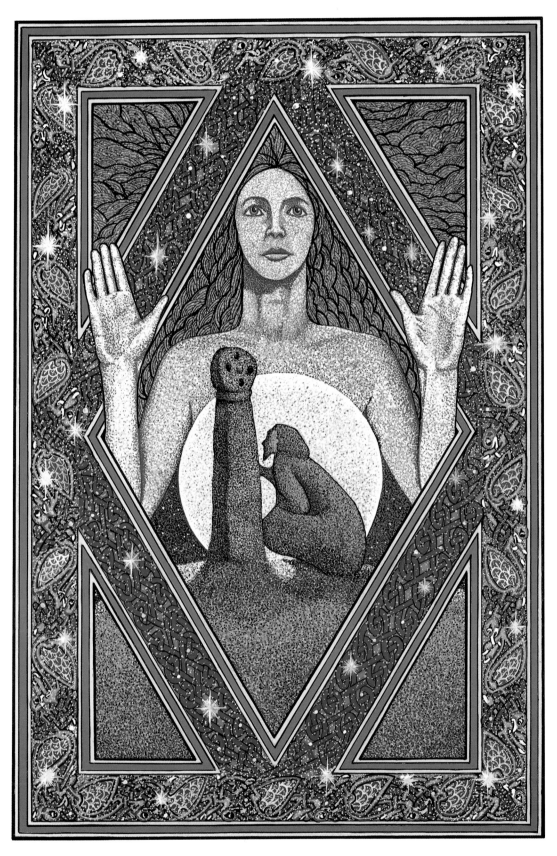

'Celtia' (1988)
the fusion of pagan and Christian belief

The New Way

As political Christianity began to spread through Europe in the 2nd century AD it attempted to adapt many of the obstinately held old beliefs. Festivals of the seasons were given the names of Christian saints or other holy people. Pope Gregory instructed Augustine that, if pagan beliefs could not be easily discarded, then they should be turned into Christian practices. God was implicitly male; this tended to reduce the status of

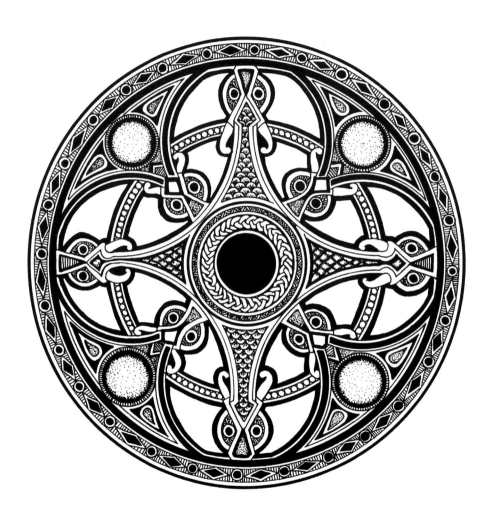

women, who came to have no role within the priesthood. Things went out of balance – those with any understanding of sacred herbs and potions or psychic gifts came to be frowned upon and persecuted by the Church authorities. Almost to compensate, Mary, the mother of Jesus, became known as the mother of God and began to absorb many characteristics of the Earth Mother Goddess. In symbolism, Christ became associated with the sun, while Mary became associated with the moon.

'The Fusion' (1992)
based on the Strickland brooch, 9th century AD

Brighid and St Bride

One of the most important of the Celtic deities, Brighid's memory is still celebrated in folklore and Celtic tradition today as Bride or Brigid.

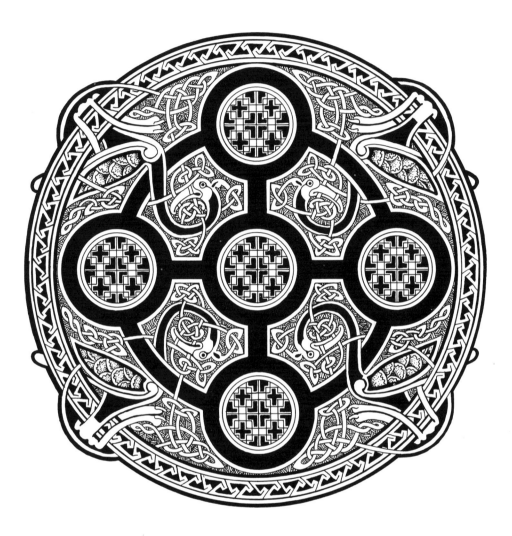

The observance of the perpetual fire where she was worshipped at Kildare in Ireland suggests the possibility that the monastery there may have had links with druidic practices.

Brighid's dwelling place was said to radiate light, as if on fire, and to this day she is remembered as Bride, the patron saint of the family hearth.

In the highlands of Scotland prayers are uttered to St Bride to facilitate childbirth, because it was believed she had travelled to Bethlehem as midwife to Mary when she gave birth to Jesus.

'The Cross of Friendship' (1992)

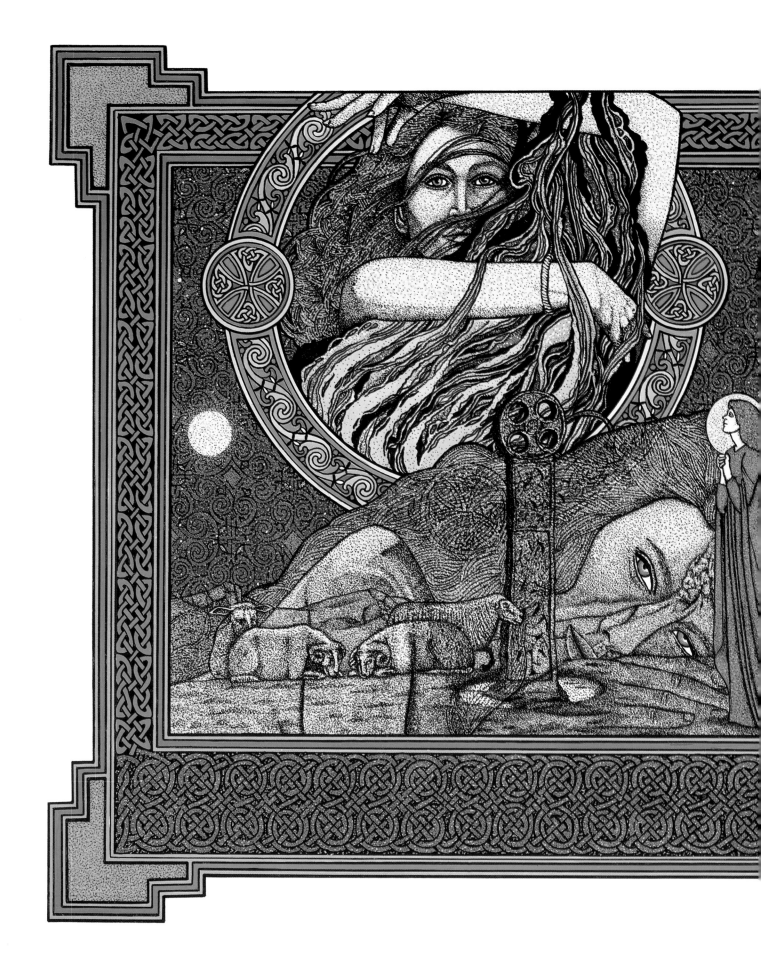

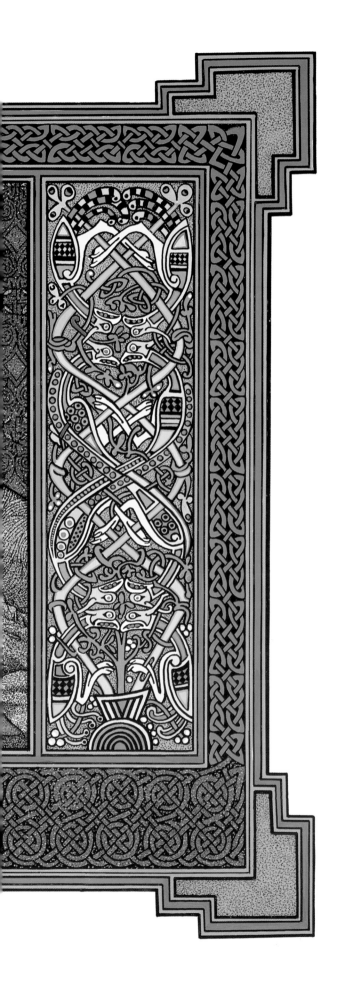

Brighid represented the sister or virgin aspect of the Great Goddess and was associated with fire, the home, caring for animals and sacred wells.

In her triple form she has two sisters who were patronesses of therapy and metalwork or smithing.

'The Triple Goddess' (1990)

CELTIC ARCHETYPES

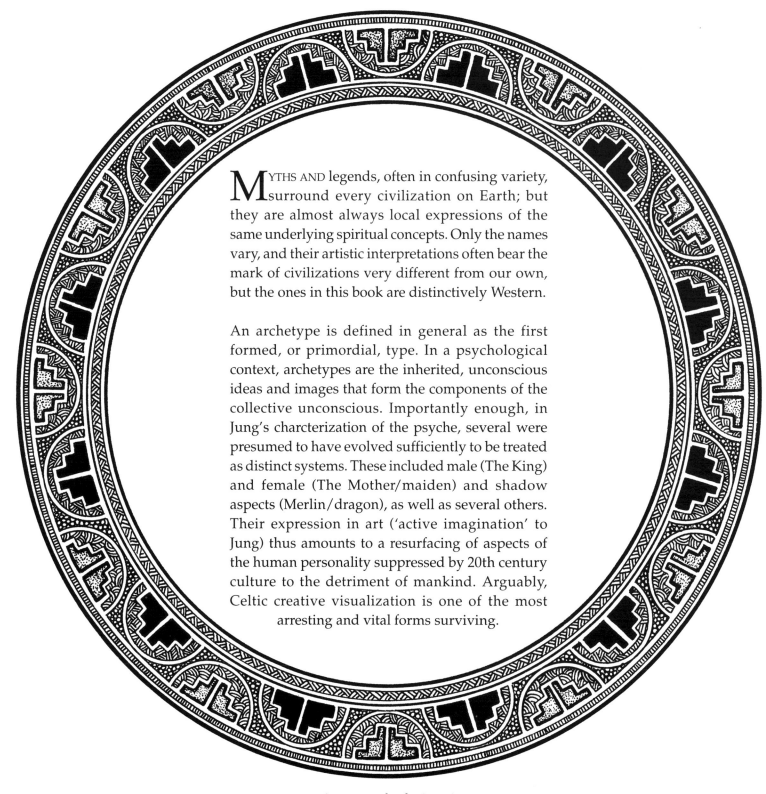

MYTHS AND legends, often in confusing variety, surround every civilization on Earth; but they are almost always local expressions of the same underlying spiritual concepts. Only the names vary, and their artistic interpretations often bear the mark of civilizations very different from our own, but the ones in this book are distinctively Western.

An archetype is defined in general as the first formed, or primordial, type. In a psychological context, archetypes are the inherited, unconscious ideas and images that form the components of the collective unconscious. Importantly enough, in Jung's charcterization of the psyche, several were presumed to have evolved sufficiently to be treated as distinct systems. These included male (The King) and female (The Mother/maiden) and shadow aspects (Merlin/dragon), as well as several others. Their expression in art ('active imagination' to Jung) thus amounts to a resurfacing of aspects of the human personality suppressed by 20th century culture to the detriment of mankind. Arguably, Celtic creative visualization is one of the most arresting and vital forms surviving.

Step pattern border (1992)

To the extent that every man has a feminine side to him, and every woman a male side, as well as all the other, often conflicting intangible components of personality, including good and evil, these can be manifested as myths and legends containing inner truths of tremendous force. To illustrate courage, for example, it is easiest to tell a story – any story will do that conveys the idea of the principle in action, as opposed to the abstract concept.

Celtic myth and legend is a particularly rich vein of such striking stories, with characters corresponding strongly to archetypes identified by Jung. This helps to explain the continuing fascination with King Arthur, for example, and symbols or images associated with him.

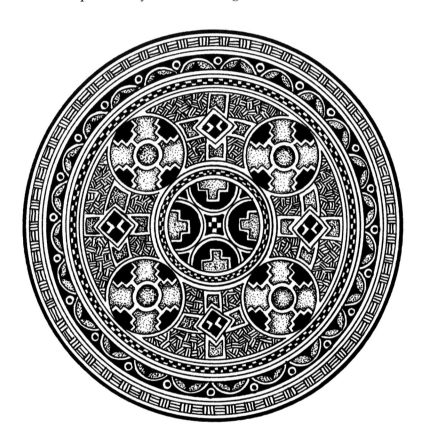

Scientific materialism hates what cannot be observed or measured, and has tended to feel uncomfortable with what it sees as primitivism. Yet the thing persists. In movies like *Batman*, *Robin Hood* and *Dancing with Wolves* ancient chords are struck that echo in the box office.

What is so exciting about Celtic myth? Mainly that it is the living primordial myth of an evolved people, ourselves. Arguably, the Celtic archetypes have been passed on from this first major European civilization by ancestry and intermarriage.

'The Motionless Mover' (1992)

TALIESIN

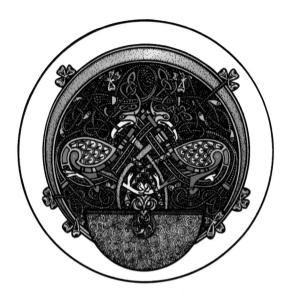

Cerridwen
and the Birth of Taliesin

The Great Goddess of the ancient world had three aspects – the crone, the mature woman and the maiden, who were in turn also each in a triple form. Cerridwen, a Welsh crone, was keeper of the cauldron of the underworld, in which spiritual knowledge and darker visions were brewed. She had a daughter, Crearwy, who represented the light side of the goddess, and a son, Afagddu, who was the dark and ugly side.

Cerridwen was preparing a special brew for her son and set a boy called Gwion to watch over the cauldron. She told him that the pot should not cease to boil for a year and a day, and that on no account was he to taste what was being prepared. Near the end of the year three drops suddenly spat out and landed on Gwion's finger. He quickly put his finger into his mouth to ease the burn, and swallowed the magical liquor.

Suddenly he was able to foresee everything that was to come, and in fear of Cerridwen finding him he fled. Cerridwen, discovering the cauldron which had now broken in two and caused the potion to pour out and be lost, pursued Gwion. During the chase they each changed into various animals and birds. Finally Gwion in desperation turned into a grain of wheat, whereupon Cerridwen transformed herself into a high-crested black hen and swallowed him.

'The Cauldron of the Underworld' (1992)

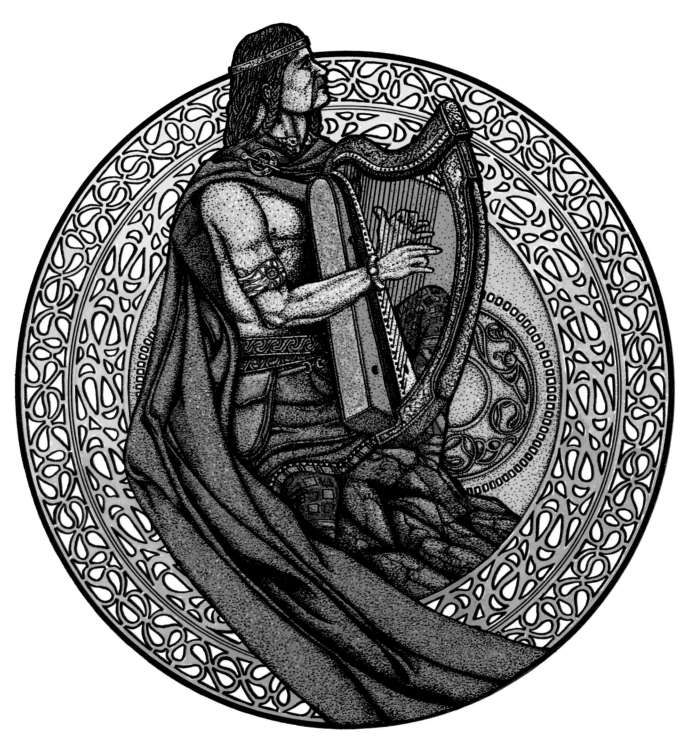

Nine months later Cerridwen gave birth to a beautiful child whom she could not find it in her heart to kill, so she wrapped him in a leather bag and cast him into the sea. The bag was discovered by Elphin, who on opening it discovered the shining forehead of a little boy and said: 'Behold, a radiant brow!', which in Welsh is Taliesin. He was to become the greatest of Welsh poets.

'Taliesin' (1992)

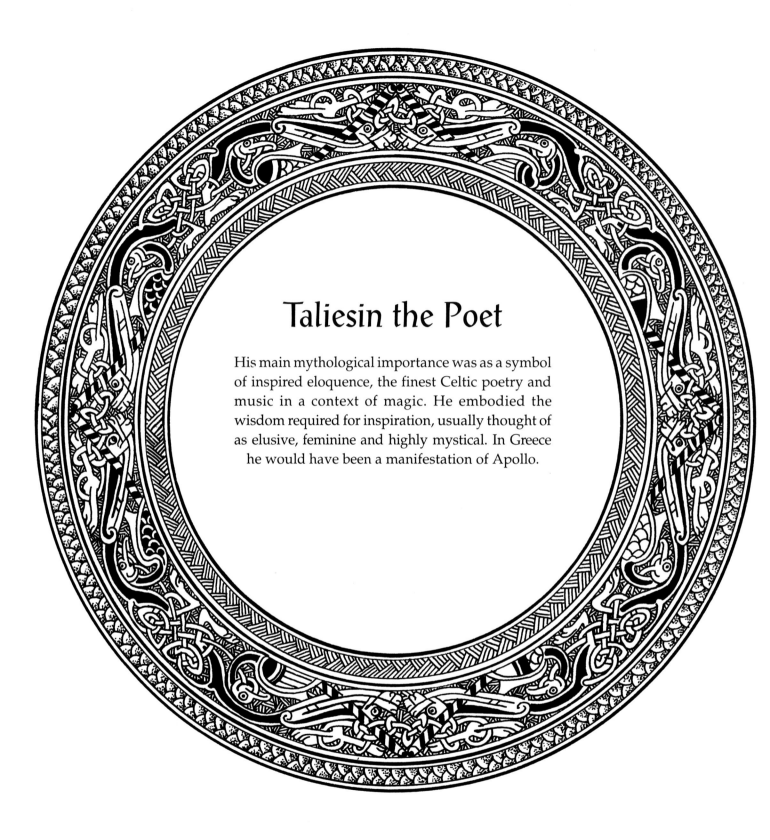

Taliesin the Poet

His main mythological importance was as a symbol of inspired eloquence, the finest Celtic poetry and music in a context of magic. He embodied the wisdom required for inspiration, usually thought of as elusive, feminine and highly mystical. In Greece he would have been a manifestation of Apollo.

'The Circle of Experience' (1992)

Taliesin's
Song of His Origins

Firstly I was formed in the shape of a handsome man,
in the hall of Cerridwen in order to be refined.
Although small and modest in my behaviour,
I was great in her lofty sanctuary.

While I was held a prisoner, sweet inspiration educated me
and laws were imparted me in a speech which had no words;
But I had to flee from the angry, terrible hag
whose outcry was terrifying.

Since then I have fled in the shape of a crow,
since then I have fled as a speedy frog,
since then I have fled with a rage in my chains,
- a roe-buck in a dense thicket.

I have fled in the shape of a raven of prophetic speech,
in the shape of a satirizing fox,
in the shape of a sure swift,
in the shape of a squirrel vainly hiding.

I have fled in the shape of a red deer,
in the shape of iron in a fierce fire,
in the shape of a sword sowing death and disaster,
in the shape of a bull relentlessly struggling.

'The Knotwork Gateway'
(1992)

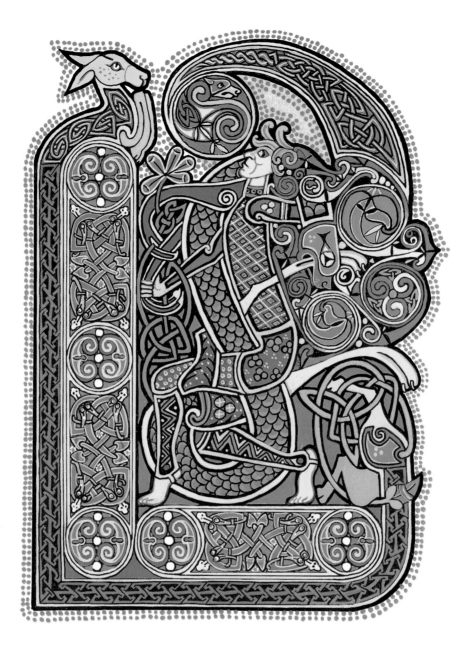

I have fled in the shape of a bristly boar in a ravine,
in the shape of a grain of wheat.
I have been taken by the talons of a bird of prey
which increased until it took the size of a foal.

Floating like a boat in its waters,
I was thrown into a dark bag,
and on an endless sea, I was set adrift.

Just as I was suffocating, I had a happy omen,
and the master of the Heavens brought me to liberty.

From *Taliesin*

'Challenge' (1985)
painting for **Celtic Art of Courtney Davis**

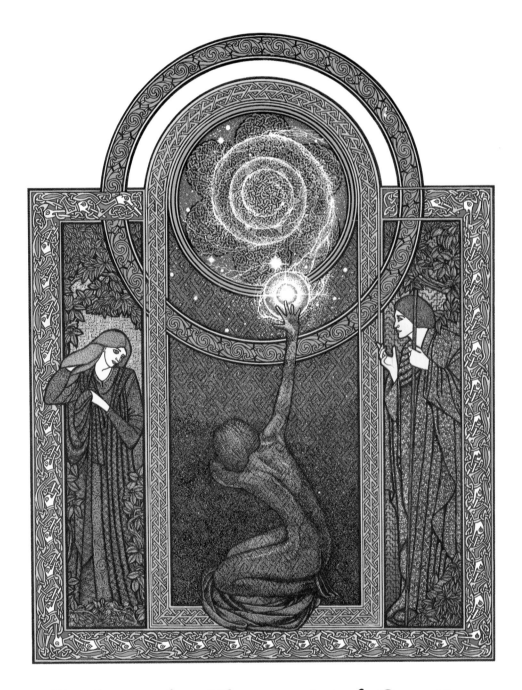

Oath to the Elements of Creation

May the earth open and swallow me,
May the sky fall upon me,
May the seas rise and cover me,
May fires consume me,
If I am forsworn.

From *Taliesin*

'The Oath to the Elements of Creation' (1989)

CELTIC GODS AND HEROES

The *Lebor Gabala*, the *Book of Conquests*, tells of six successive waves of invaders arriving in Ireland. The Irish identified themselves with the Tuatha De Danaan, children of the goddess Danu. The greatest of all the warriors was the Sun God Lugh, who fought the eternal battle with darkness. The Tuatha De Danann came from the mythical north, the traditional location of magic, and were skilled in druidic lore. In battle they used wonderful weapons with superhuman powers to overcome foes such as the Fomhoire, who were one-eyed demons.

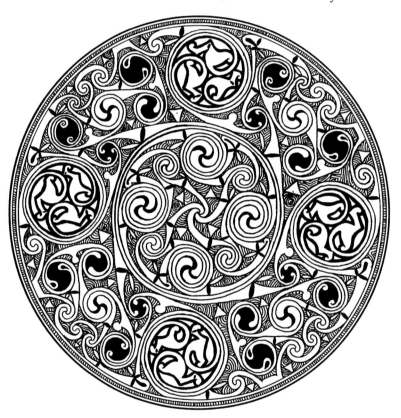

Eventually the Tuatha De Danann were defeated by the sons of Mil – the Gaels or humans. This happened when their champion Cuchulainn failed to recognize the Morrigan, the War Goddess who then deprived the Tuatha De Danann of her aid. It was resolved that the sons of Mil should inhabit the outerworld, while the Tuatha De Danann should dwell in the lower realms of the earth below the mounds of fairy sidh. These Neolithic barrows were thought of as fairy dwellings and there are still strong traditions in Ireland which preserve the idea of a magical people who live below ground.

'The Still Centre' (1992)

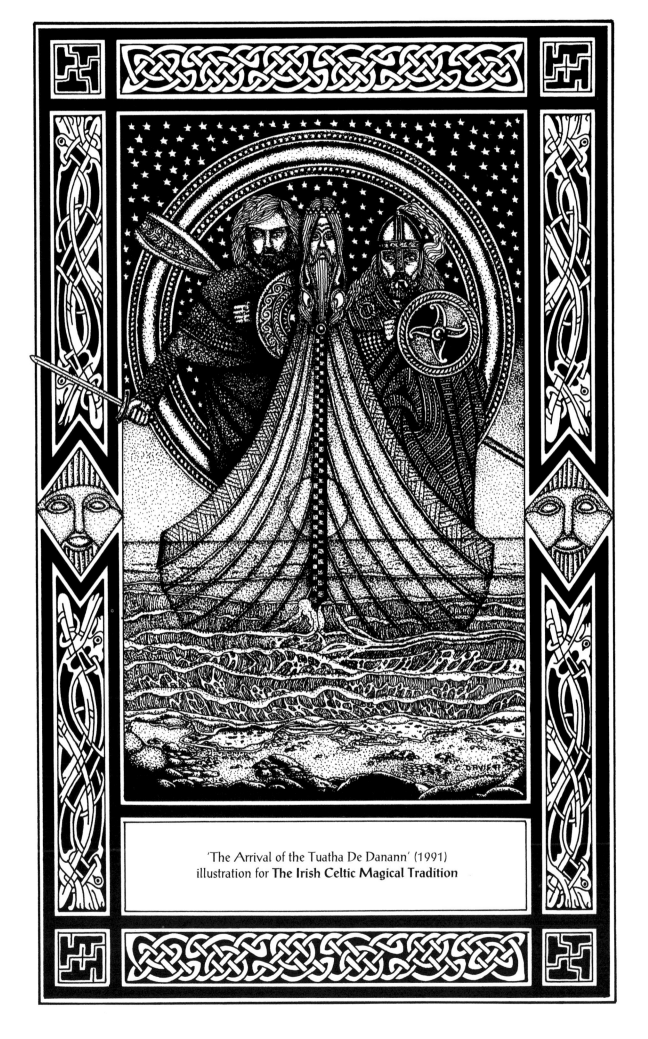

'The Arrival of the Tuatha De Danann' (1991)
illustration for **The Irish Celtic Magical Tradition**

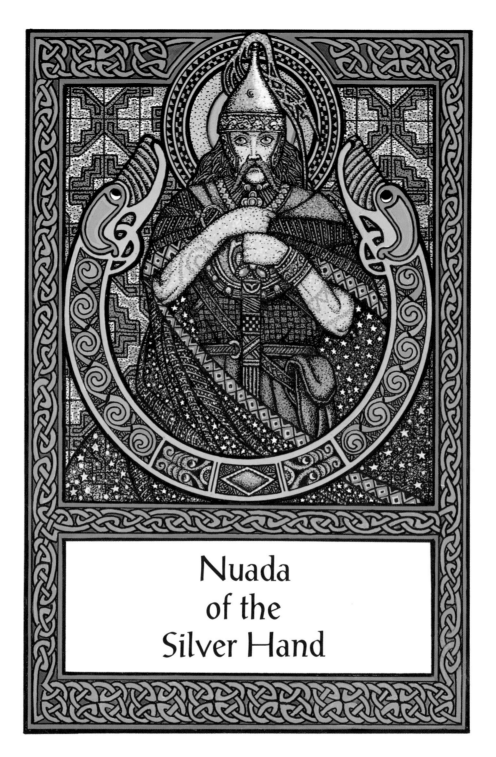

Nuada
of the
Silver Hand

Nuada Argatlam, the king of the Tuatha, was a major deity of the Celts and, like Daghdha and Nuada, one of the 'father' gods. In his keeping was the magical sword of Nuada, one of the treasures of the Tuatha De Danann; when it was unsheathed, no enemy could escape it. In the first battle of Moytura Nuada lost his hand, which was subsequently replaced by one of silver. But this injury deprived him of his kingship, as only physically perfect men were allowed to hold the office of king.

'Nuada of the Silver Hand' (1991)
cover for **The Irish Celtic Magical Tradition**

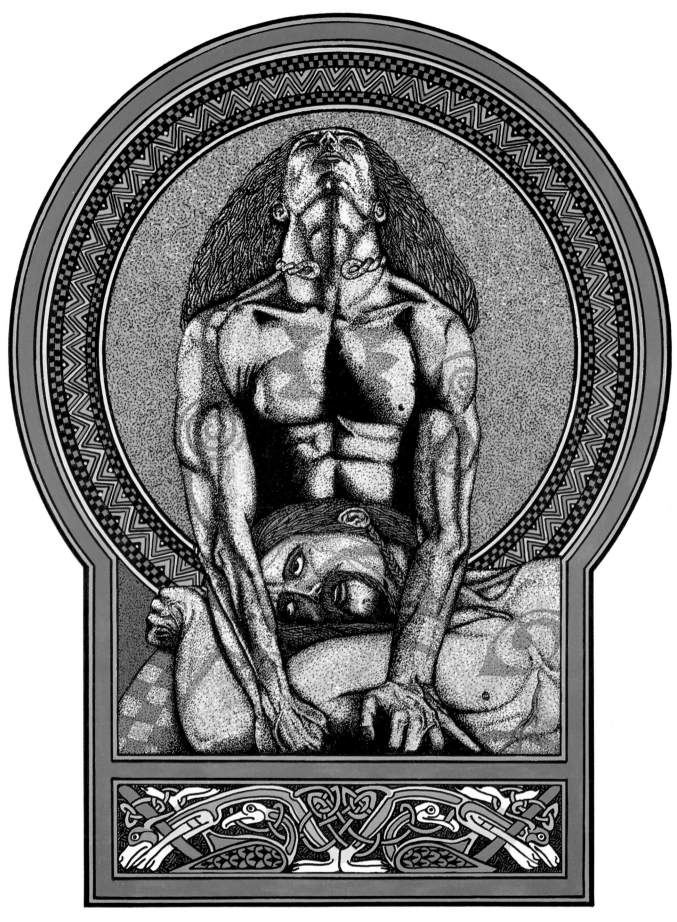

'The Radiant Warrior' (1992)

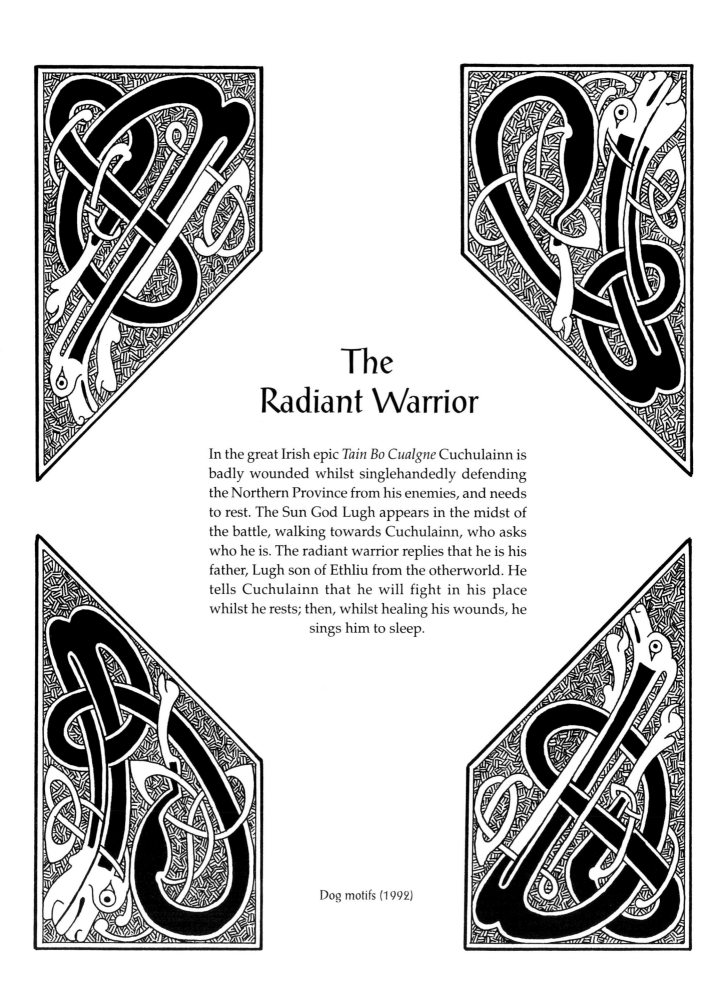

The
Radiant Warrior

In the great Irish epic *Tain Bo Cualgne* Cuchulainn is badly wounded whilst singlehandedly defending the Northern Province from his enemies, and needs to rest. The Sun God Lugh appears in the midst of the battle, walking towards Cuchulainn, who asks who he is. The radiant warrior replies that he is his father, Lugh son of Ethliu from the otherworld. He tells Cuchulainn that he will fight in his place whilst he rests; then, whilst healing his wounds, he sings him to sleep.

Dog motifs (1992)

The Lament of Queen Maev

1. Raise the Cromlech high!
   Mac Moghcorb is slain,
   And other men's renown
   Has leave to live again.

2. Cold at last he lies,
   'Neath the burial stone.
   All blood he shed
   Could not save his own.

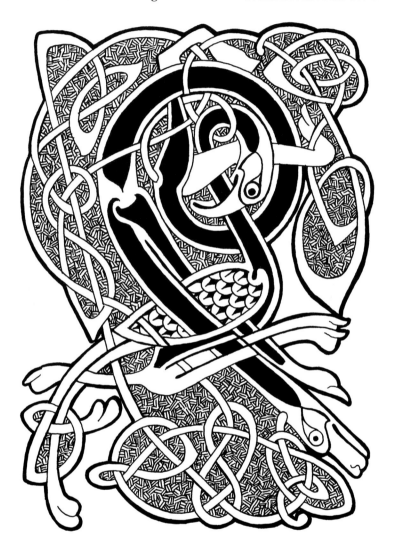

3. Razor-sharp his spear,
   And the shield he bore,
   High as champion's head –
   His arm was like an oar.

4. Terror went before him,
   Death behind his back,
   Well the wolves of Erinn
   Knew his chariot's track.

5. Seven bloody battles
   He broke upon his foes,
   In each a hundred heroes
   Fell beneath his blows.

6. At the Boundary Stream
   Fought the Royal Hound,
   And for Bernas battle
   Stands his name renowned.

7. Here he fought for Leinster
   Last of all his frays –
   On the hill of Cucorb's Fate
   High his Cromlech raise.

Ancient Erse (shortened version),
author unknown

Dog and bird motif (1992)

THE GREAT MAGICIAN
AND THE
SOLAR KING

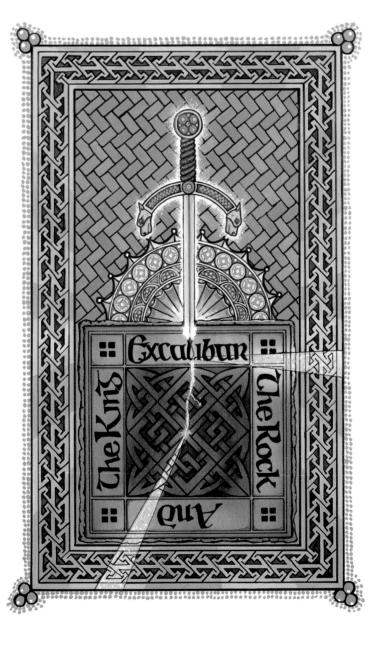

THE CELTIC cultural and spiritual tradition is encapsulated in the Arthurian legends and Merlin's transformation from an extraordinary boy into a seer and mentor of the new solar archetype.

It is now believed that Arthur may well have been an historical figure living in the 6th century AD. The earliest documents refer to him as the leader of the Britons who mounted a series of battles against the invading Saxons. But it is Arthur's importance as a mythical solar warrior, and Merlin's as the archetype of superior wisdom, that make the stories live on today.

'Excalibur, the Rock and the King' (1986)

The Portrait of Merlin

Surmounting the illustration are two aspects of Merlin: on the right, the archdruid or magician receiving the divine light or Awen; on the left, the returned or risen Merlin holding in his palm the first of the seven stars of the Plough (the other six stars of this constellation are hidden elsewhere in the painting).

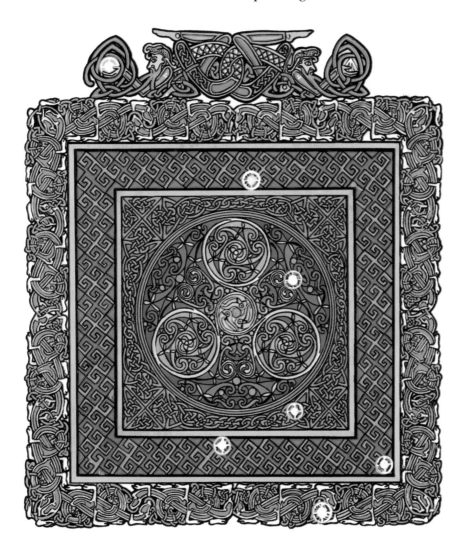

The knotwork outer border represents the Wheel of Rebirth or, in this instance, Merlin's progress from the physical form, with which most of us associate him, towards a state of pure being. The maze-like inner border signifies the path of initiation. The spiral patterns near the centre of the picture chart this journey through physical life, death and rebirth, and on into the finer realms of existence beyond. As we draw closer to the omphalos, the central meeting point of heaven and earth, other kindred forces merge with the spirit of Merlin.

'Portrait of Merlin' (1987)

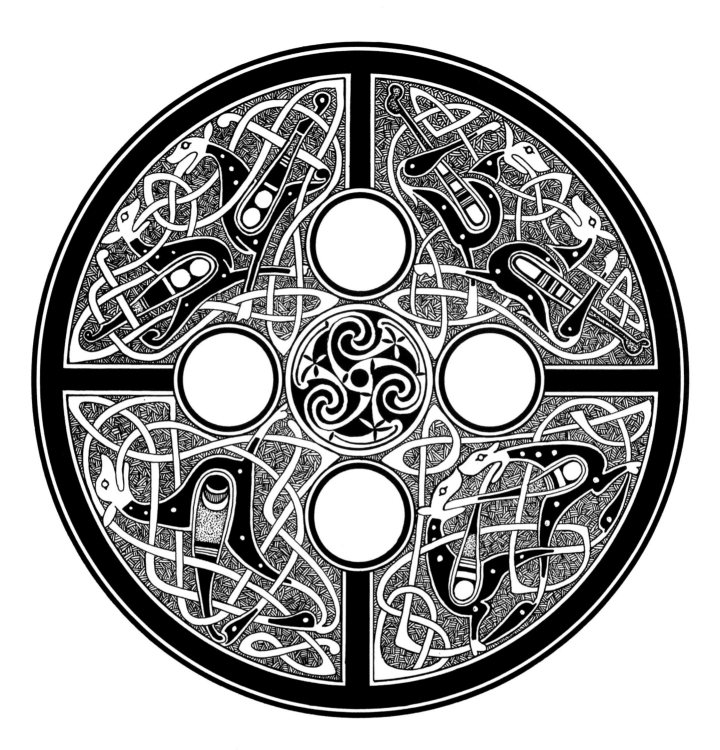

Consider how Will, Love, Wisdom and Intelligence unify and sustain all things, from the dance of the smallest electron to the majestic procession of the galaxies.

How could it be otherwise?

From *Merlin the Immortal*

Design taken from one disc of a triple pin set
dated 8th century AD (1991)

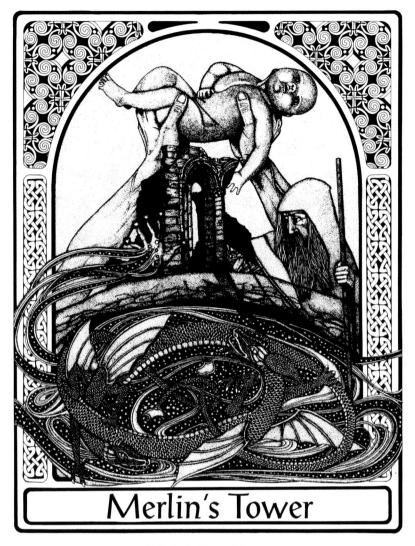

'Merlin's Tower' (1991)
illustration for **The Encyclopedia of Arthurian Legends**

It is through the writings of Geoffrey of Monmouth in the 12th century and Malory in the 15th century, which were drawn from Celtic sources, that the court of Arthur came to life. In these works Merlin achieves his fullest development as a character who used his prophetic powers and magical abilities to bring Arthur to the throne of Britain.

In the sixth book of Geoffrey of Monmouth's *Histories of the British Kings* there is an account of the British ruler Vortigen, who had conspired with the invading Saxons and now feared for his life. He was advised by the druids that he should build a great tower of exceeding strength on Mount Eryri – Snowdon. The task was beset with nightly interruptions, and the foundations were swallowed up by the soil by some occult force.

It was decided that a fatherless boy should be sacrificed and his blood sprinkled on the foundation stones before building was again commenced. The boy chosen was young Merlin, but before he could be sacrificed he told the king and the druids what he believed was the real cause of the disturbance in the foundations. Through visions, he saw that underneath the structure were two dragons doing battle in a cave. The ground was immediately excavated and a large pool was discovered – the lair of the two dragons. All were amazed at Merlin's vision, and he was deemed Possessed by the Spirit of God.

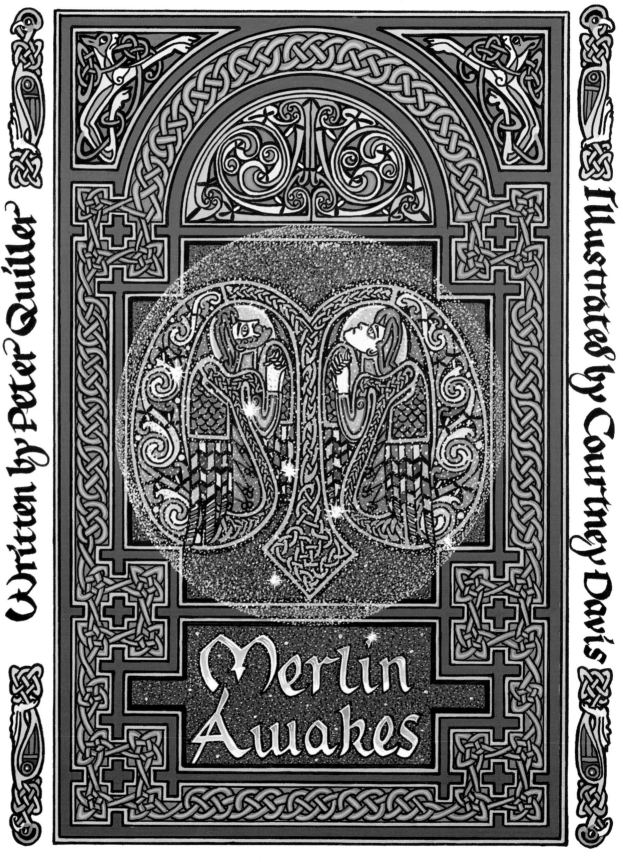

Written by Peter Quiller

Illustrated by Courtney Davis

Merlin Awakes

Proposed cover for **Merlin Awakes**

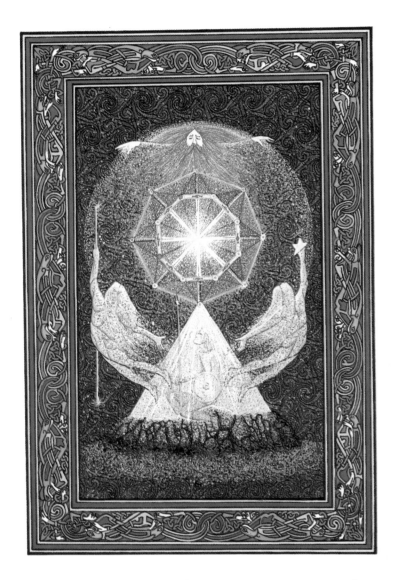

Merlin, the Essence of Celtic Consciousness

Merlin also represents the continuity of Celtic wisdom across time. He is the bridge that links the old order with newer ones, the essence of Celtic consciousness that manifests itself in new forms appropriate to their time. So long as that essence lives (and it is as strong today as it ever was), the Spirit of Celtia will play an important part in human life.

From *Celtic Art in the Northern Tradition*

'Merlin, an Aspect of the Great Magician' (1987)

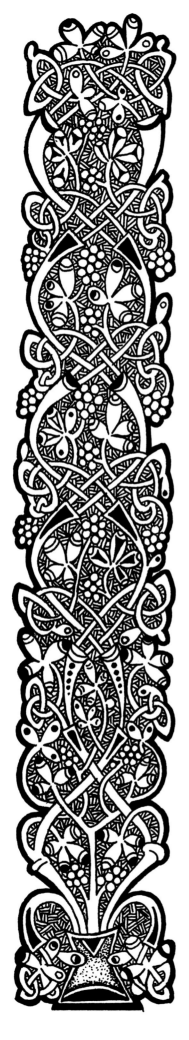

Merlin the Immortal

In 1974 I went through a series of experiences which totally changed the direction of my life. It was not until I was asked by a friend to produce a portrait of Merlin in 1984 that I understood who had been pulling my strings over the years. The only help my friend would give me for my task was to tell me to look to the Plough in the sky for guidance. So one night I stood outside my home at Reading in Berkshire and looked up at the night sky. With – I must admit – some embarrassment in case I was overheard, I asked Merlin's help. No sooner had I muttered his name under my breath than a shooting star flew through the centre of the pattern of stars, followed by the faintest laughter in my ears. I had discovered Merlin.

Over the following months, I had some meetings with another friend, Peter Quiller, who had had similar experiences with Merlin. He and I set about producing a book which eventually became *Merlin the Immortal* and was later republished in a new edition in 1988 as *Merlin Awakes*.

'The Tree of Great Joy' (1992)

84

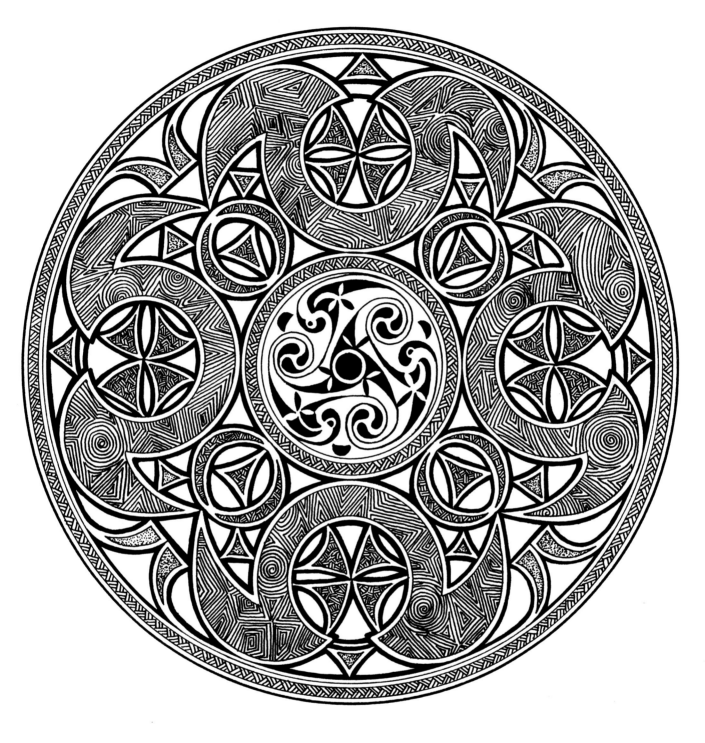

It is your destiny one day to join us.
One day, like us you will guide younger worlds.
And so it goes on in a perfect spiral.

From *Merlin the Immortal*

'Celtic Magic' (1992)
based on a 5th century BC openwork bronze disc

Many great Truths are staring you in the face –
the Kingdom of Heaven is all around you,
you have only to open your eyes.

From *Merlin Awakes*

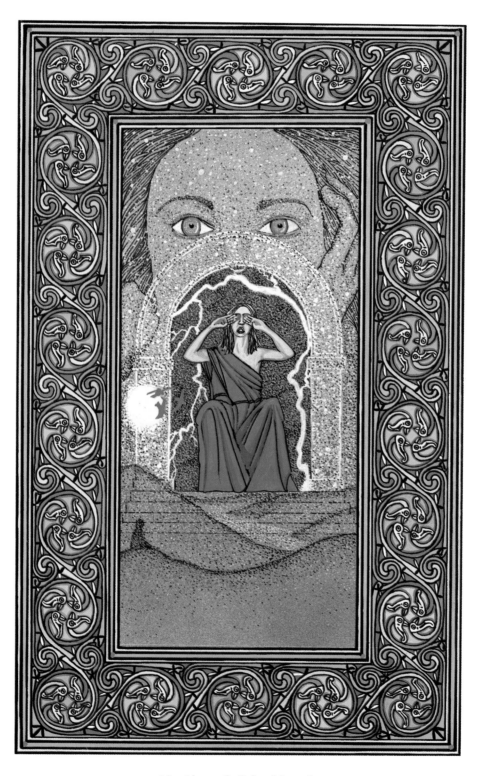

'As Above, So Below' (1985)

I need to watch the sun, to calculate the hours that I should pray to God. But the blackbird who nests in the roof of my hut makes no such calculations: he sings God's praises all day long.

From *Celtic Fire*

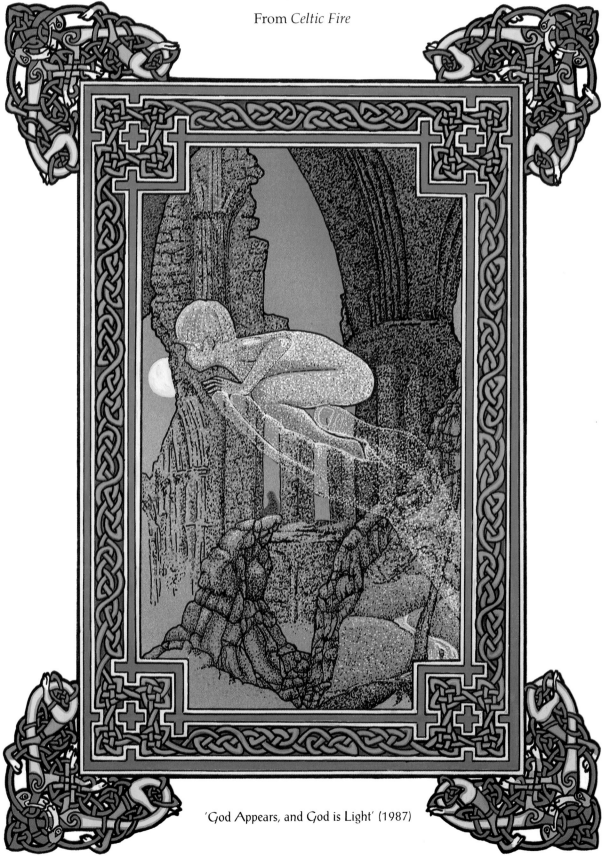

'God Appears, and God is Light' (1987)

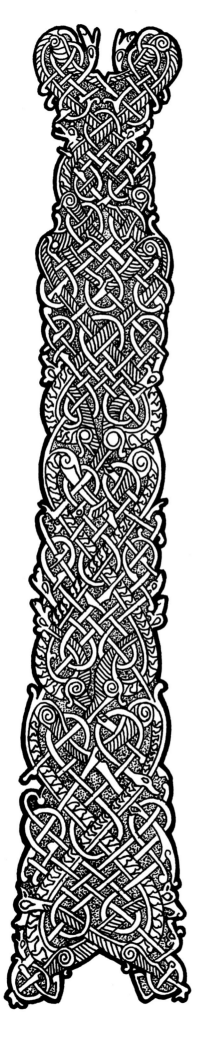

Arthur

Ever inventive, and seeing spiritual dictators for what they were and always have been, writers in the older tradition evolved the incredibly sophisticated Arthurian and Grail stories in a Christian context. These persist to the present day and are metaphors for spiritual and psychological development, respecting the Universal Feminine conveniently provided by the then fashionable idea of courtly love. In fact, they are the coded messages of a Mystery school, and survive because of the power of their hidden messages.

The Grail is the goal of wholeness in the human psyche, while Merlin is the archetype of superior wisdom. The knights can be seen as different aspects of the human personality; Arthur represents the state of overall awareness itself. And so on.

The universality of the archetypes is shown in the breadth of appeal of this series of myths, which also worried theologians of all Christian sects. Arthur and his Knights were Christian Celts of the 6th century . . . weren't they? At worst they seemed to be romantic fiction unworthy of life's learned and life's wise. Or were they really the finest Western expression of universal spiritual values and the techniques of their development in a tradition feared by the authorities, spiritual and temporal? Feared because it put overwhelming value on the individual's direct experience of God, to whom he was really responsible, and on his own conscience. The Celts' most trying trait was their fierce love of the truth. It still is.

Today it would be called individuation – the process of becoming an individual who is aware of his or her own identity as opposed to that imposed by the collective norms of society. Such people are dangerous.

Detail from the Cross of Cong (1992)

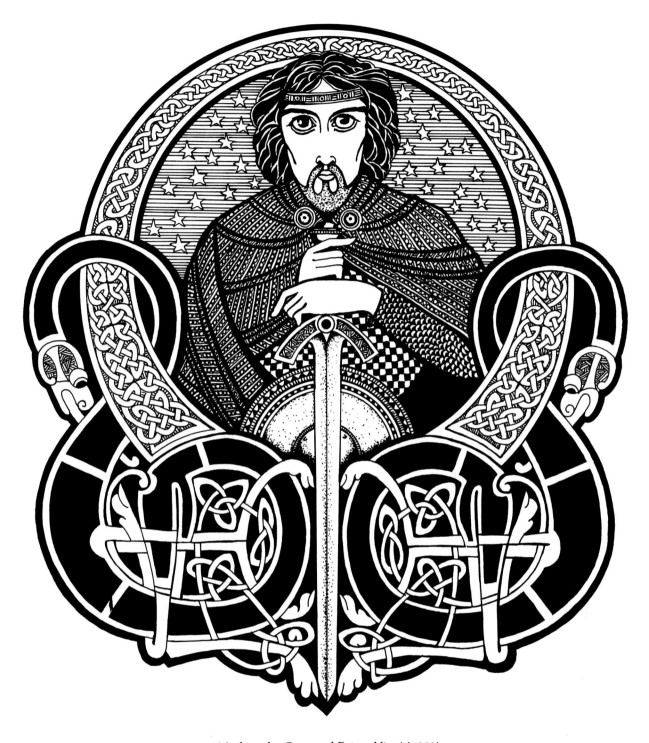

'Arthur, the Once and Future King' (1992)

The process also involves acknowledging both the masculine and feminine within ourselves, and the Celts held these two opposing principles in real balance – indeed, implicit in the Celtic cross is the concept of the transcendent union of equal opposites. These are the principles of reason and emotion, rational and the irrational, male and female. The symbols of each are combined to form a transcendent third. Latin crosses bear no circle.

The ideal that this represents goes directly against today's ethos of the worship of reason and intellect alone, and is its antidote. Respect the feminine in ourselves, and we respect the Earth. For best results, hold the rational and irrational in balance, as did the Celts. Images in this book are a contemporary visual expression of the psychological symbols they employed to make abstract ideas real and compellingly magical.

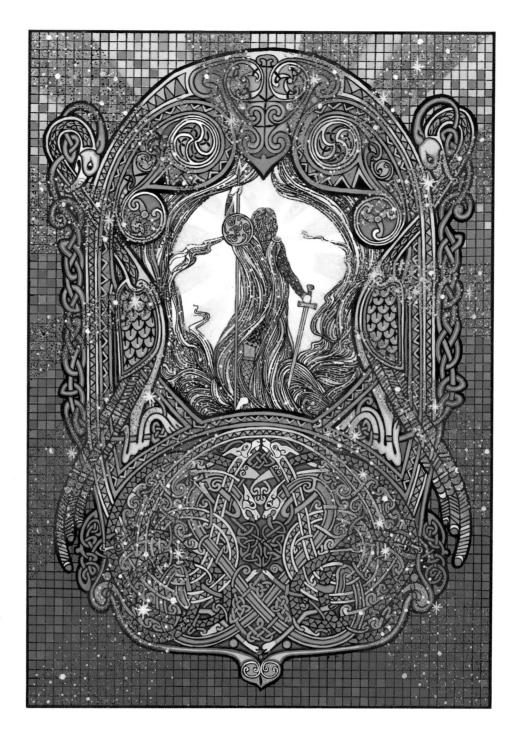

The easy movement between the human warrior hero and his other-wordly archetype, the Sun God, is a common practice in every kind of Celtic story.

From *Celtic Mysteries*

'Stepping into the Otherworld' (1987)

The Glass Isle

The legendary dish with which the Saviour is said to have celebrated the Last Supper with his apostles, the Holy Grail, has a long history within the Arthurian traditions. There are many stories of the sacred vessel being brought to Britain by Joseph of Arimathea after Christ's crucifixion.

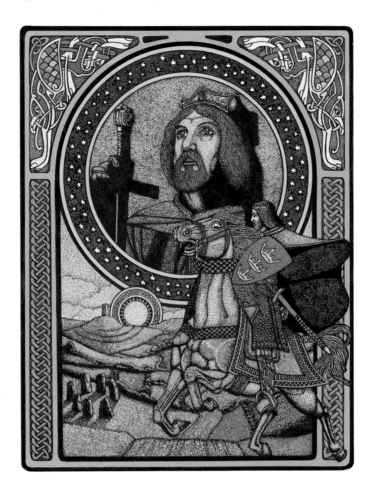

In fact the concept of a sacred receptacle hidden at Glastonbury may derive from the much older folk legend of a magical cauldron belonging to a Celtic fertility cult. In the early 13th century an anonymous author wrote a book entitled *Grand St Graal*, describing Joseph's arrival on this island which was then languishing in darkest paganism. Some of the inhabitants were converted to Christianity, but others refused and were destroyed in a flood. Above their bodies a tower was built, known as the Tower of Marvels, over which, it was prophesied, a king named Arthur should reign. Other legends tell how on arriving at Glastonbury, formerly known as Ynis Witryn, or the Island of Glass, Joseph of Arimathea and his followers built a wattle church in which to teach people the true faith.

'Glass Isle' (1991)
cover for **The Encyclopedia of Arthurian Legends**

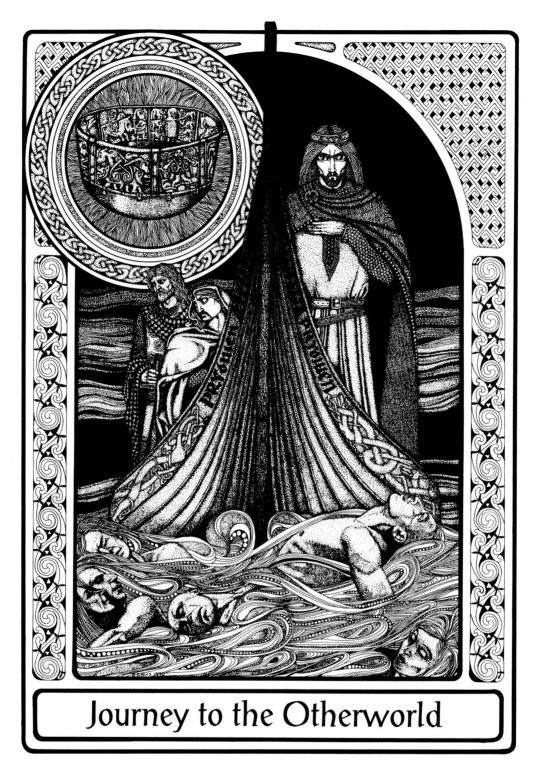

Journey to the Otherworld

In an early Celtic poem, *The Spoiling of Annwn*, the Welsh poet Taliesin narrates the expedition of Arthur the Solar King and his company of divine heroes, who sail into the supernatural otherworld in his boat Prydwen to carry off the magic cauldron of inspiration and plenty. In later, Christianized stories this theme was attached to the search for the Holy Grail, the vessel which carried the blood of the Redeemer.

'Journey to the Otherworld' (1991)
illustration for **The Encyclopedia of Arthurian Legends**

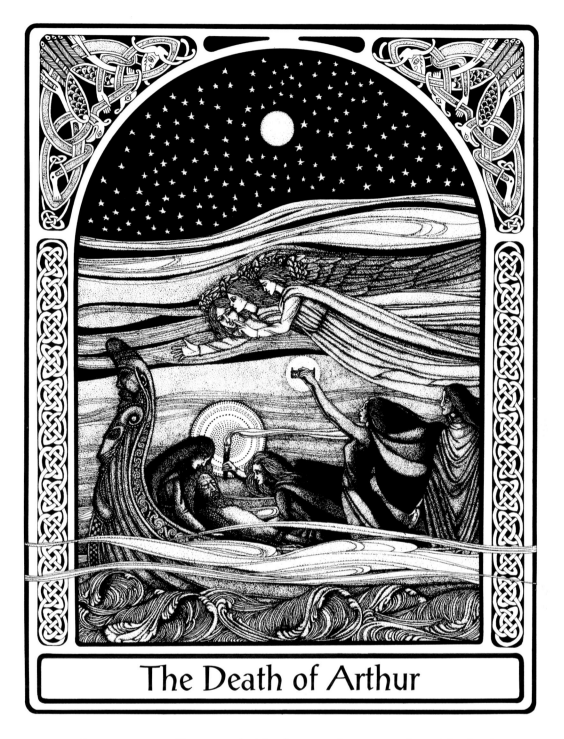

The Death of Arthur

Arthur was mortally wounded by his treacherous nephew Mordred at the battle of Camlan.

In the *Vita Merlini* Geoffrey of Monmouth tells us that Merlin and the Welsh bard Taliesin took the stricken Arthur to Avalon, the Fortunate Island, where he would be cured of his deadly wounds by the goddess Morgan and her nine sisters, who were able to heal the incurable and prophesy the future.

'Death of Arthur' (1991)
illustration for **The Enclyclopedia of Arthurian Legends**

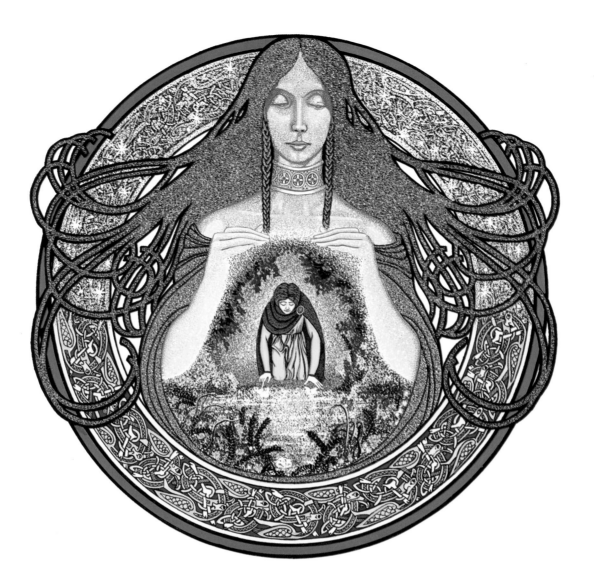

The Mother

The story of Perceval's quest for the Holy Grail is stronger in the French and German romances than in the English Arthurian tradition, but importantly it is his mother who played a key role in establishing the background for his quest; her over-protective nature and his isolated home delayed his natural development. Queen Herzeleide (meaning 'Heart Sorrow') deliberately chose her woodland home to protect him from the hazards of the outside world and the fate of her husband and brothers, who died fighting for chivalric causes. Her nest protection instinct was justified when Perceval was young and helpless, but she maintained it too long and his childlike innocence become a liability. In psychological terms she is the classic mother figure of the unconscious from whom the individual spirit must break free, much in the same way as the seed of a plant has to break out of the earth to blossom.

'The Mother' (1989)
painting for **Symbols of the Grail Quest**

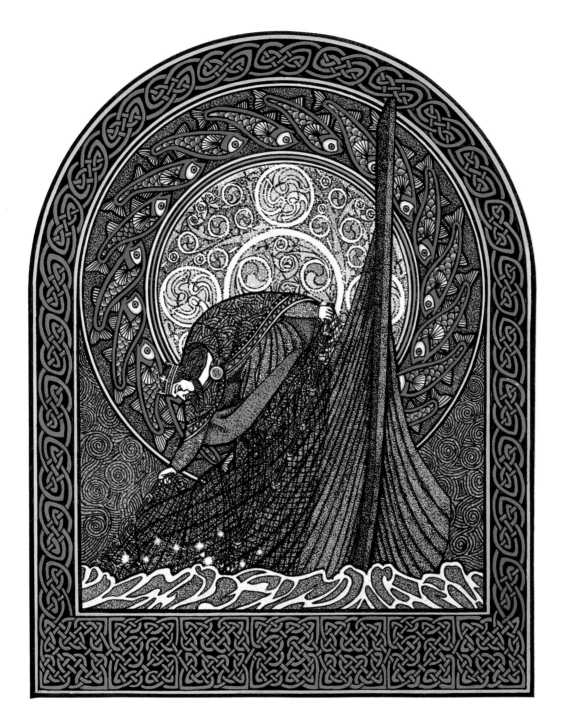

The Grail King

In Christian terms the Rich Fisher is forever casting his net in an endeavour to draw the realization of Christ from the depths of inner man. In psychic terms he can be said to be trying to draw the sparkling facets of individuality from the formless sea of the unconscious.

From *Symbols of the Grail Quest*

'The Grail King' (1989)

The Dialogue of Arthur and Eliwood

An encounter between the great warrior Arthur and his nephew Eliwood, who has been reborn in the shape of an eagle.

Arthur
I behold a wonder, bardic,
Sitting high among oaken branches,
Is this the vision of an eagle, or an illusion?

Eagle
Arthur, of great fame,
Strength and power to your host.
This is an eagle that you see.

Arthur
I wonder at your being here,
And will ask you, in metre,
What is the vision of an eagle?

Eagle
Arthur, whose fame is widespread,
Whose host is of brilliant aspect,
This eagle have you seen before.

Maze border (1992)

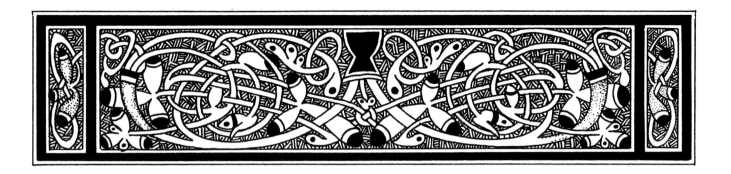

Arthur
Eagle, being on top of the oak,
If you are of the race of birds,
Are you domestic or tame?

Eagle
Arthur, great portent,
Before whose onset nothing stands,
I am the son of Madoc ap Uthyr.

Arthur
I know not this kind of eagle,
Frequenting the vales of Cornwall.
Madoc ap Uthyr is dead.

Eagle
Arthur of fierce and subtle speech,
Whose host is uncurtailed wrath,
I was Eliwood.

Arthur
Eagle of blameless aspect,
Whose discourse is sweet,
Are you Eliwood my nephew?

Eagle
Arthur, audacious in the onset,
If I am Eliwood
Am I welcome here?

Arthur
Eagle, true of speech,
If you are Eliwood
Was the slaughter good around you?

Eagle
Arthur, audacious of answer,
Before whom no enemy stands,
From death there is no escape.

From *Taliesin*

'The Celtic Tree of Life' (1992)

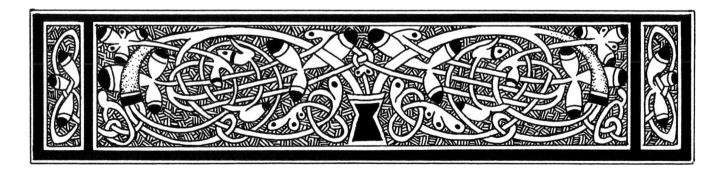

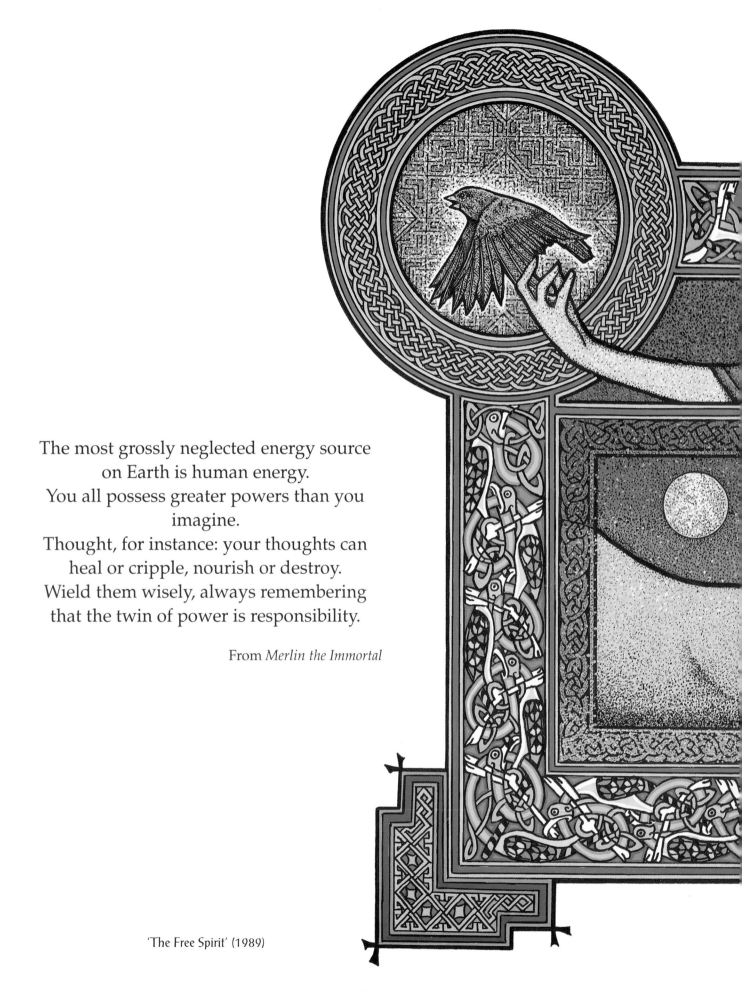

The most grossly neglected energy source
on Earth is human energy.
You all possess greater powers than you
imagine.
Thought, for instance: your thoughts can
heal or cripple, nourish or destroy.
Wield them wisely, always remembering
that the twin of power is responsibility.

From *Merlin the Immortal*

'The Free Spirit' (1989)

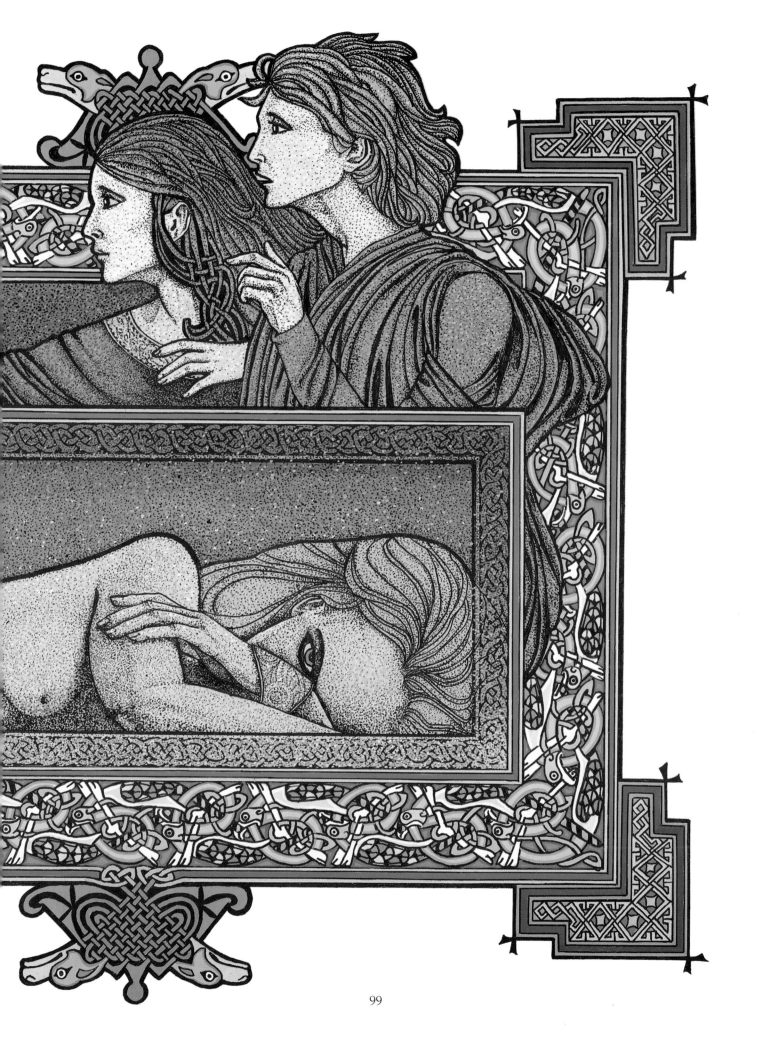

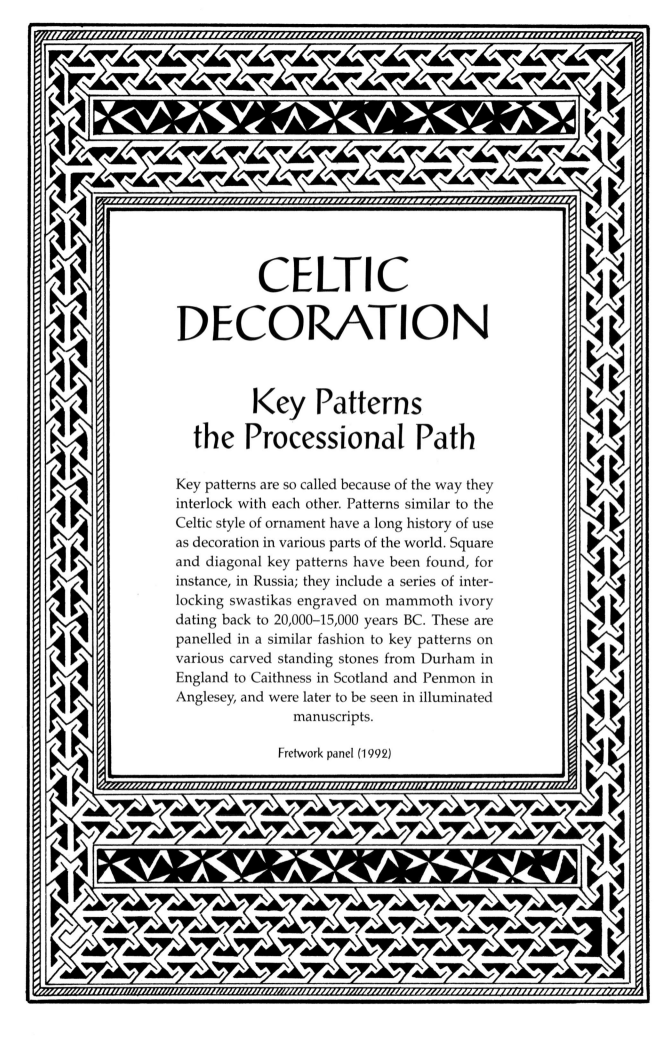

CELTIC DECORATION

Key Patterns
the Processional Path

Key patterns are so called because of the way they interlock with each other. Patterns similar to the Celtic style of ornament have a long history of use as decoration in various parts of the world. Square and diagonal key patterns have been found, for instance, in Russia; they include a series of interlocking swastikas engraved on mammoth ivory dating back to 20,000–15,000 years BC. These are panelled in a similar fashion to key patterns on various carved standing stones from Durham in England to Caithness in Scotland and Penmon in Anglesey, and were later to be seen in illuminated manuscripts.

Fretwork panel (1992)

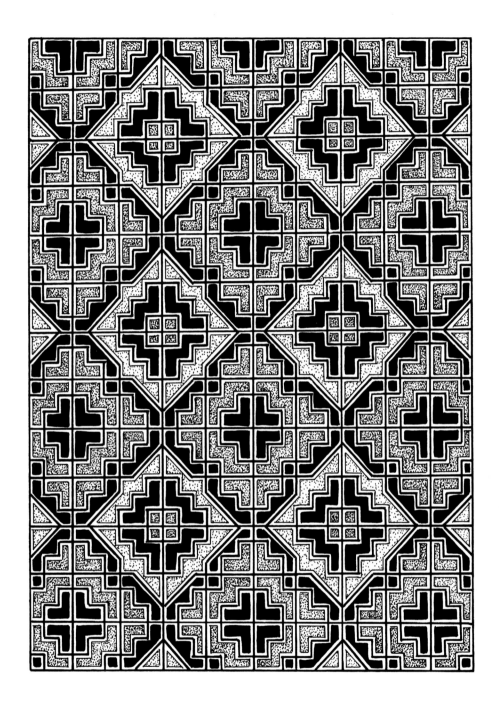

This design is based upon a step pattern created by the monk Eadfrith, which formed part of a fully decorative or cross carpet page in his masterpiece of religious art, the illuminated gospels, produced at Lindisfarne monastery in Northumbria around AD 698.

Carpet design (1992)

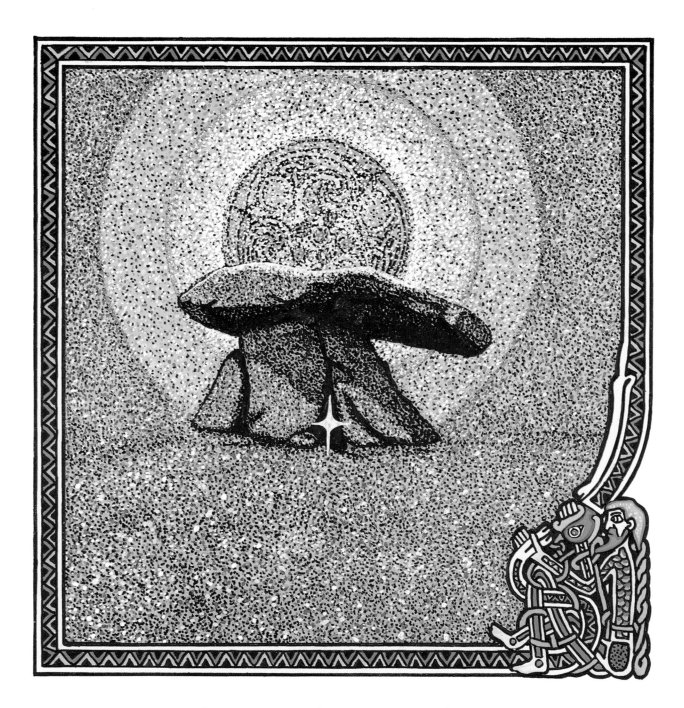

The Womb Place of the Earth Mother

Dolmens, quoits, cromlechs and caves were the burial places of the dead,
where this world and the otherworld met. The druids considered these sites
to be sources of energy, and gathered there to perform their ceremonies for
the regeneration of the land and for the wellbeing of the living.

'The Womb Place of the Earth Mother' (1988)
cover for the music tape **The Sacred Thread of Life**

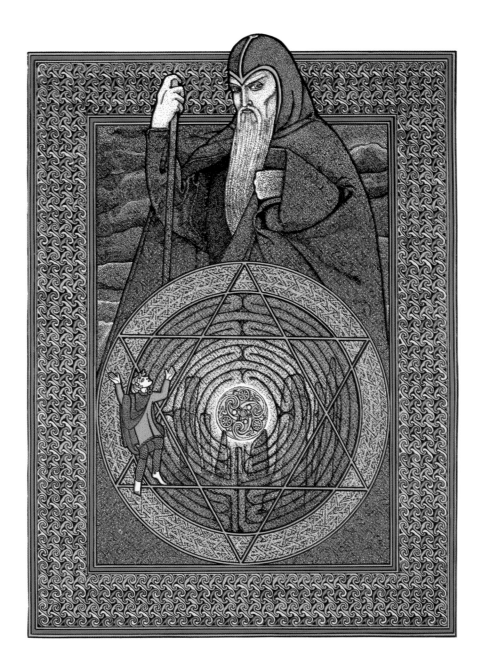

The Labyrinth

The labyrinth creates and protects the still centre, allowing entry to its knowledge only in the correct way, through initiation, once all our old ideas and preconceptions have been discarded. The magician directs our path through the labyrinth, and with each step and obstacle that we overcome the scales fall from our eyes and we see anew. For each new step we take is a reawakening to a greater knowledge and an understanding long hidden from our gaze. And though the journey may be hard, he takes our hand and leads us to the omphalos at the centre, the Cosmic Spiral that links Heaven and Earth.

'Walker on the Maze' (1988).

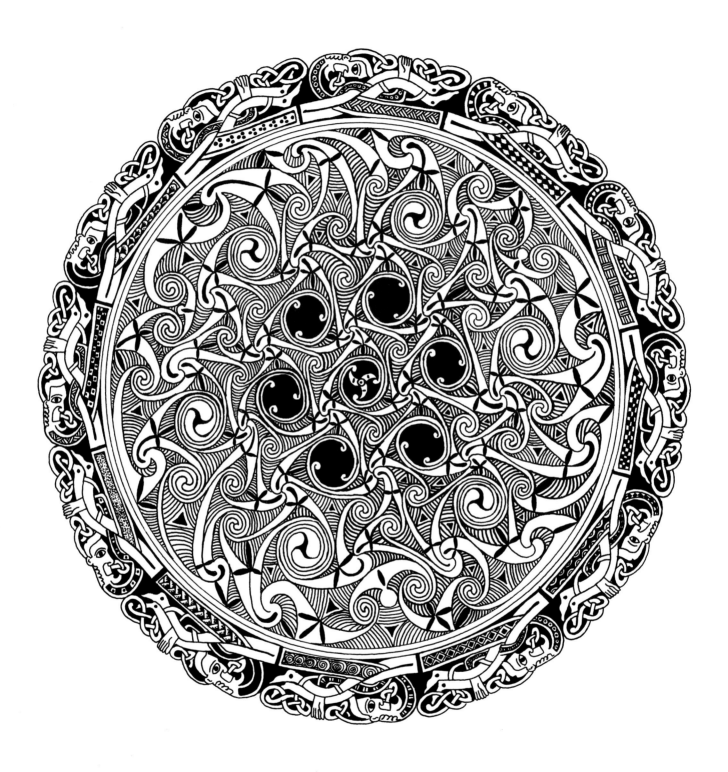

'The Great Wheel' (1992)

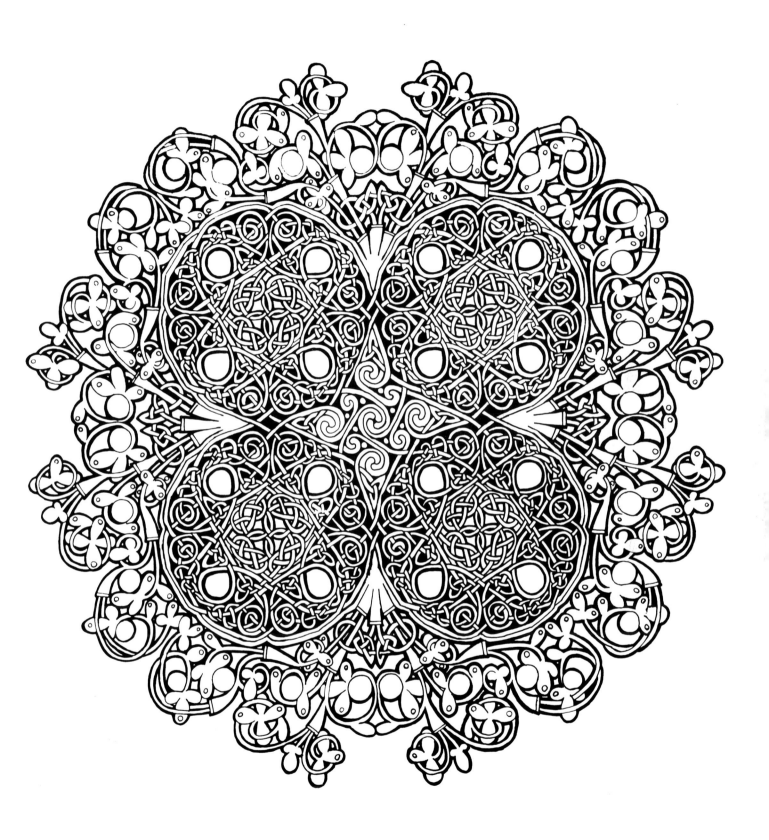

'Lifespirit' (1988)
illustration for **The Celtic Art of Courtney Davis**

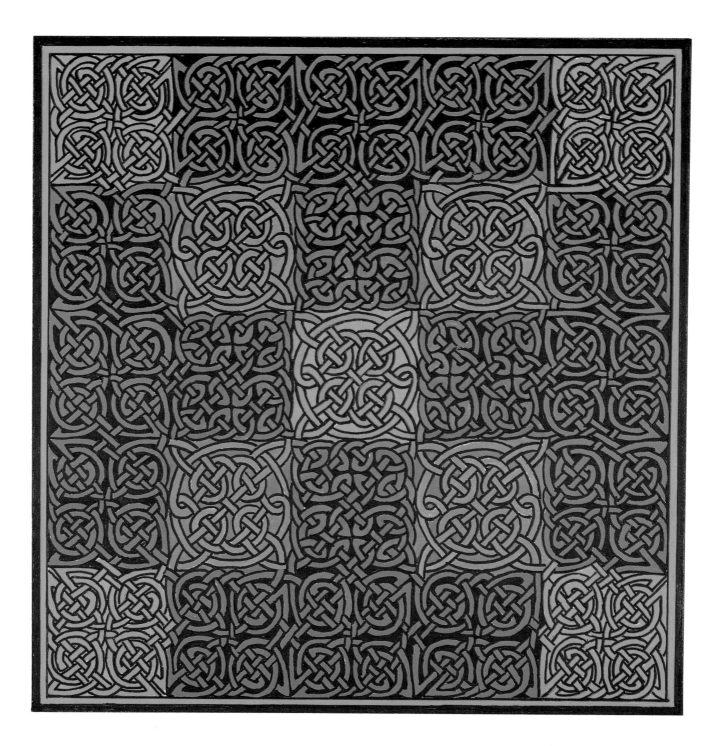

Knotwork – the Cosmic Loom

The Great Cosmic Loom of the universe symbolizes the continuity of existence of the spirit, like the continual drone maintained in the background of Celtic music – we are shown that there was never, and will never be, a time when we did or do not exist in some form.

'The Cosmic Loom' (1992)

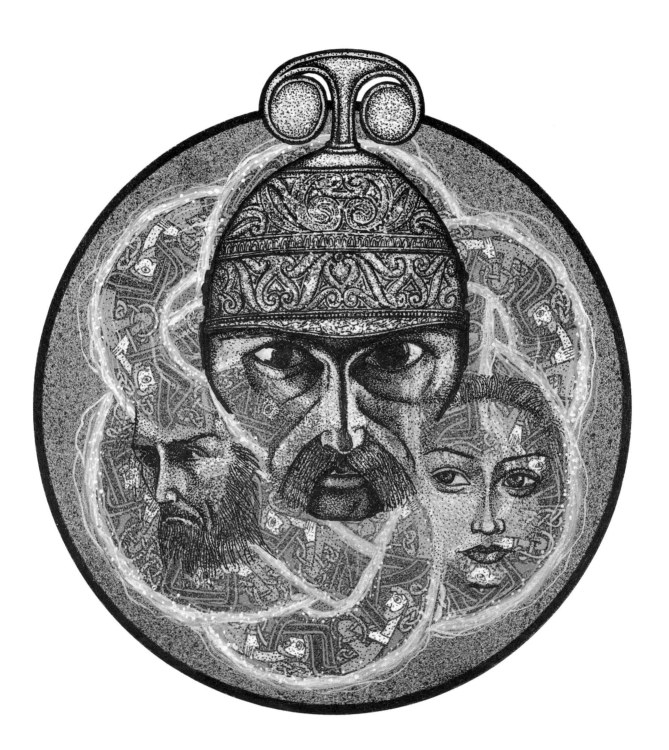

The Wheel of Rebirth

The interlace design with its unbroken lines symbolizes the binding of man's soul to the Earth. It cannot be untied until he realizes his spiritual potential and is able through his endeavours to break free of the cycle of rebirth.

'The Wheel of Rebirth' (1992)

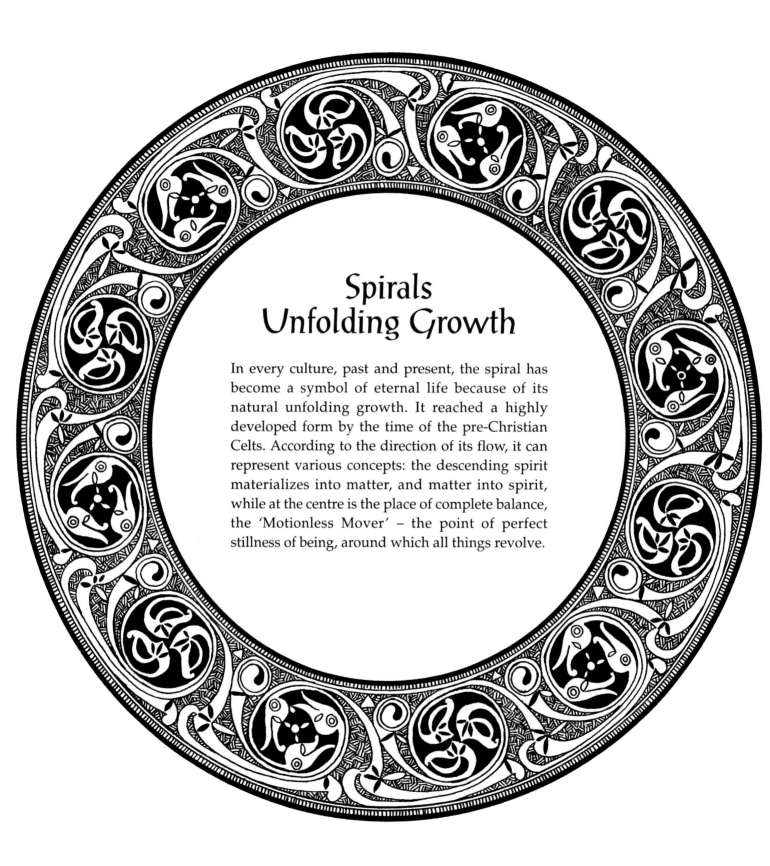

Spirals
Unfolding Growth

In every culture, past and present, the spiral has become a symbol of eternal life because of its natural unfolding growth. It reached a highly developed form by the time of the pre-Christian Celts. According to the direction of its flow, it can represent various concepts: the descending spirit materializes into matter, and matter into spirit, while at the centre is the place of complete balance, the 'Motionless Mover' – the point of perfect stillness of being, around which all things revolve.

'The Moving Spirit' (1992)

The simple spiral and two-dimensional spiral are perhaps the oldest symbols of all: they appear on megalithic monuments and cave entrances representing the continuous creation and dissolution of the world.

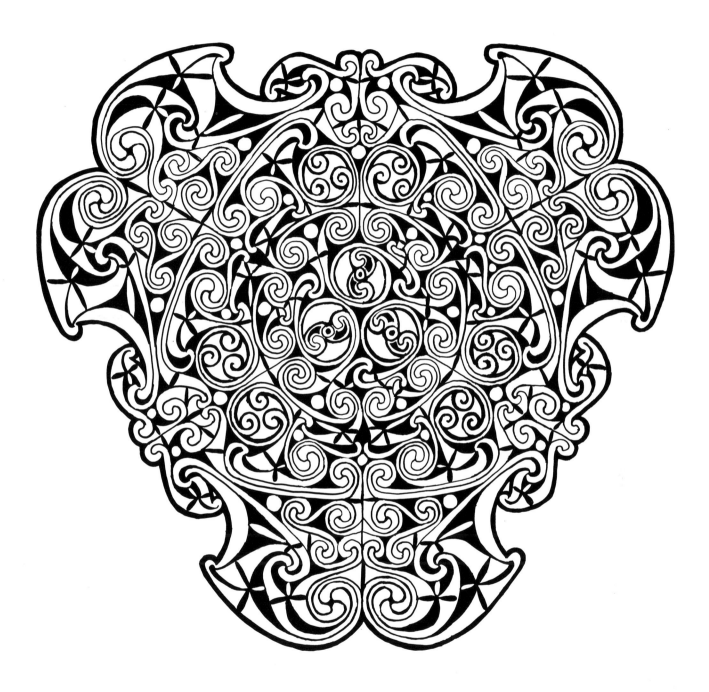

Three was a very important number to the Celts, and the three-rayed spiral known as the triskelion was widely used. It clearly related to the three- and four-rayed swastika, which represented the 'Wheel Cross'.

'The Spiral Universe' (1988)

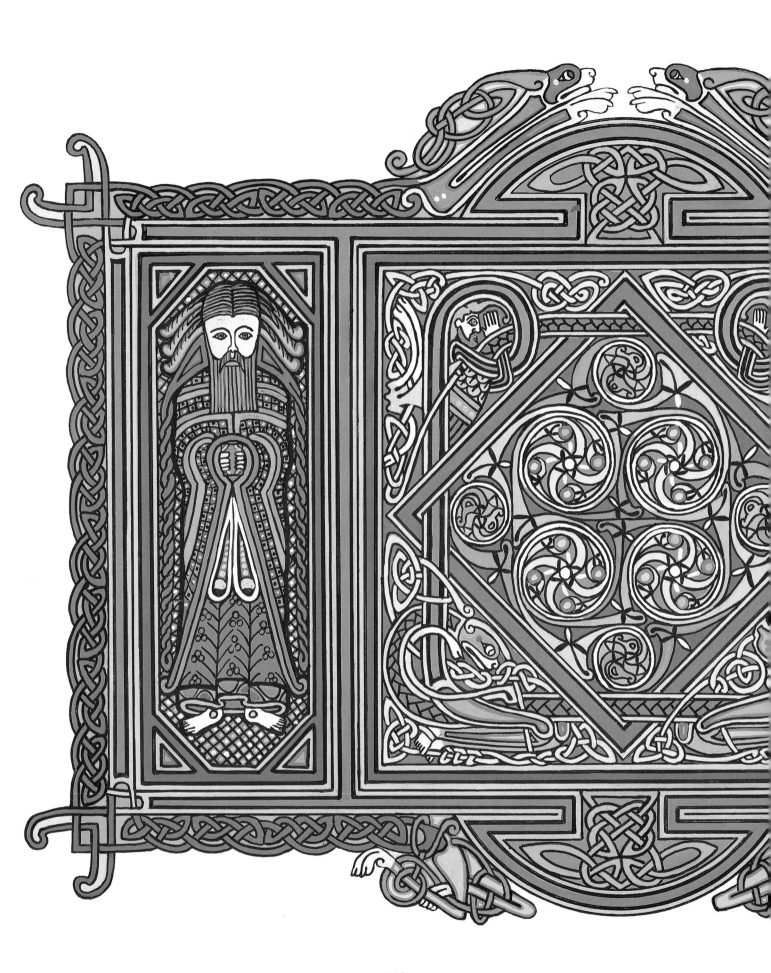

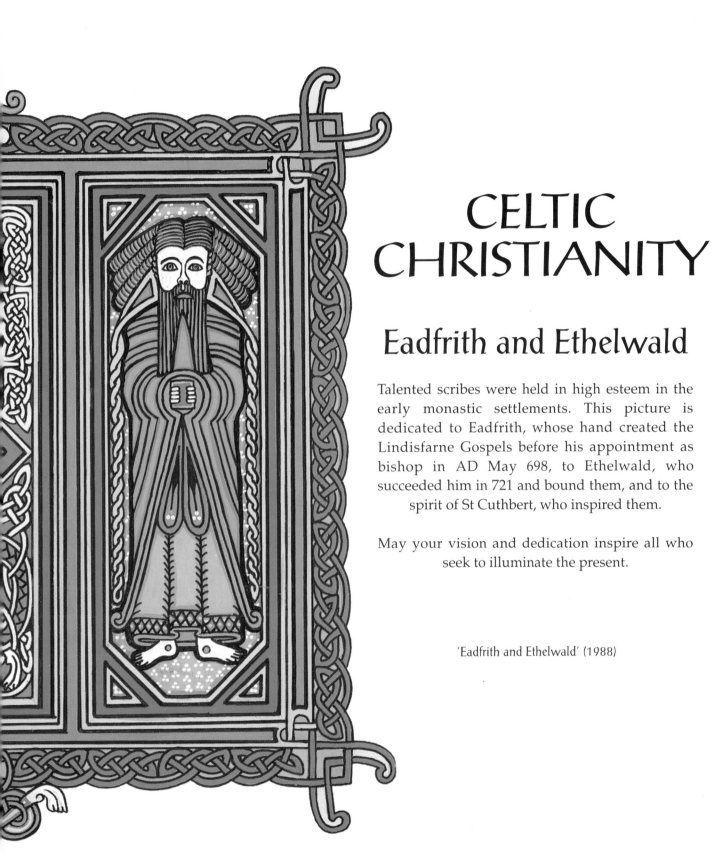

CELTIC CHRISTIANITY

Eadfrith and Ethelwald

Talented scribes were held in high esteem in the early monastic settlements. This picture is dedicated to Eadfrith, whose hand created the Lindisfarne Gospels before his appointment as bishop in AD May 698, to Ethelwald, who succeeded him in 721 and bound them, and to the spirit of St Cuthbert, who inspired them.

May your vision and dedication inspire all who seek to illuminate the present.

'Eadfrith and Ethelwald' (1988)

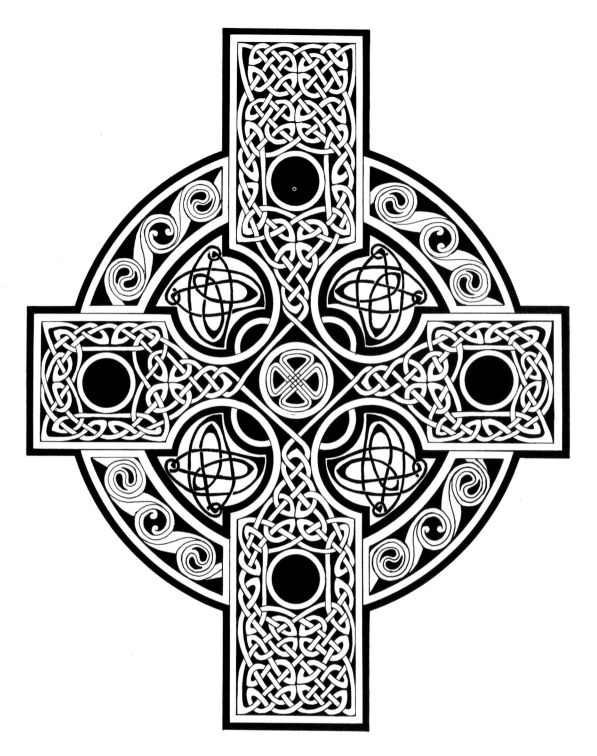

The Celtic Church

Many of the old pagan customs of worship continued to be used after
being Christianized by the building of shrines and churches on the same
sacred spots. Old gods and goddesses were renamed where appropriate,
like St Bride; others were blended with the numerous Celtic missionaries
who were deemed saints.

'The Celtic Wheel Cross' (1992)

And Did Those Feet in Ancient Times

Many legends date the early Celtic Church in Britain to at least three centuries before St Augustine, who landed here in AD 597. In the Arimathea legends we are told that Joseph built the first Christian church at Glastonbury. If other legends are to be believed, it was built on the even older site of a wattle church constructed by the boy Jesus, brought here by Joseph on one of his expeditions to buy tin, before his mission had begun.

Because of its earlier origins, the Celtic Church was entirely separate from the teachings being introduced by St Augustine. It was very much Earth-centred, poetic and mystical, and some druidic influences were still apparent: for example, the tradition of keeping a fire burning in every church and monastery as a sign of God's presence. Other differences included the date for the celebration of Easter, the rites of baptism and the ordination of bishops, which all helped to isolate the Celtic Church from the rest of Christendom.

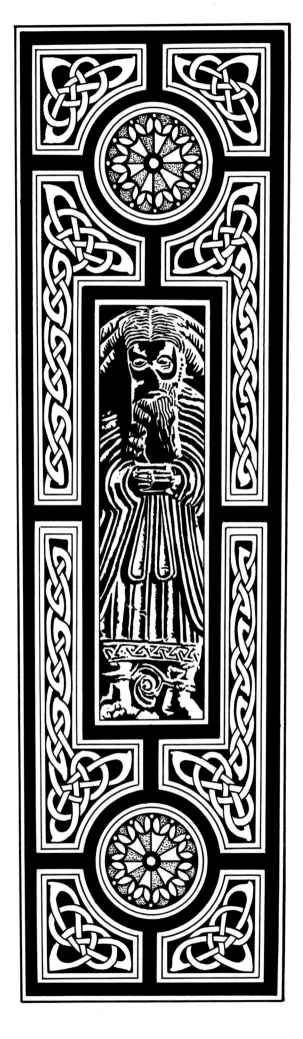

'The Silent Monk' (1991)
detail from the 11th century Breac Maodbog shrine

Thanks

to Thee O God,
that I have risen today,
To the rising
of this life itself.
May it be
to thine own glory,
O God of every gift,
And
to the glory
of my soul likewise.

From *Carmina Gadelica*

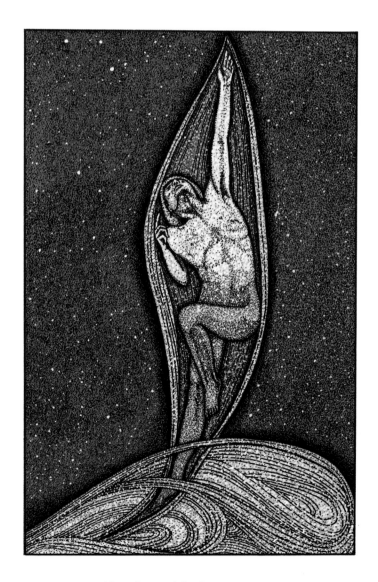

'Symphony of the Stars' (1990)

THE SAINTS

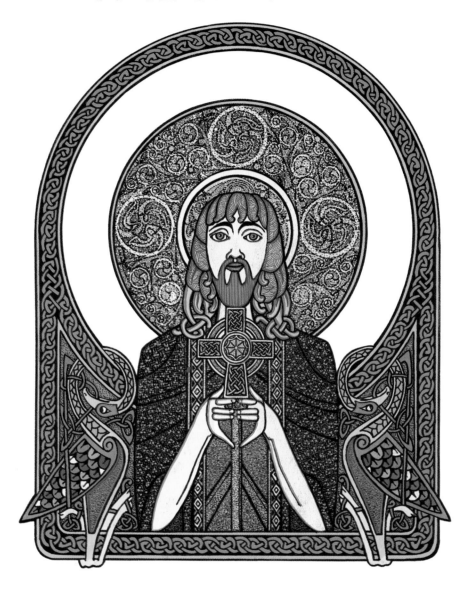

There is no Sreod that can tell our fate,
Nor bird upon the branch,
Nor trunk of gnarled oak.
Better is He in whom we trust
The King who made us all,
Who will not leave me tonight without refuge,
I adore not the voice of birds,
Nor chance, nor the love of son or wife,
My Druid is Christ, the Son of God.

'Song of Trust', attributed to St Columba, the Irish monk who founded
Iona and brought Christianity to the north of Britain

'Columba' (1988)

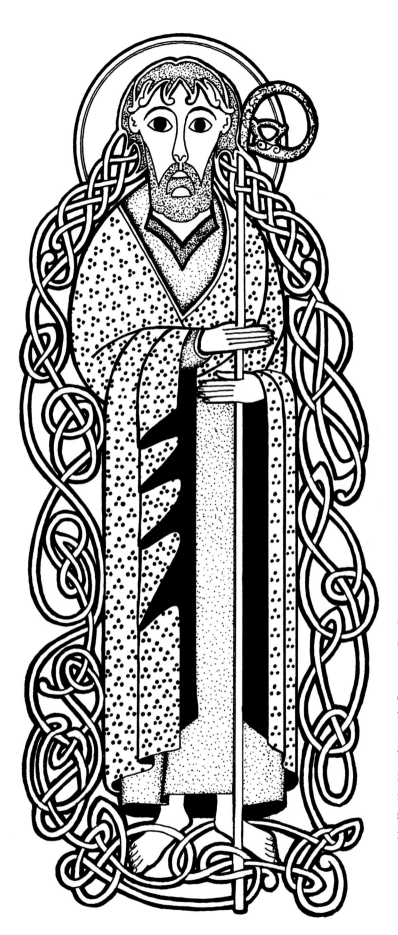

St Mungo

Mungo, whilst on his journey in search of a site to found a new monastery amongst the pagan Pictish tribesman of Scotland, came upon a wild hound who began to lead him over high mountains and deep valleys. Mungo spoke to the hound in words and the dog replied in barks and growls. Each night they lay next to each other and slept.

One day the hound stopped by a river bank and began sniffing and scratching the ground. Mungo took this as a sign from God that he should begin to build his monastery here. With great joy the missionary fell to his knees, giving thanks to God for his safe arrival. At that moment a robin swooped down on to his shoulder and kissed his neck, which Mungo took as a gesture of approval from the birds and animals.

'St Mungo' (1992)

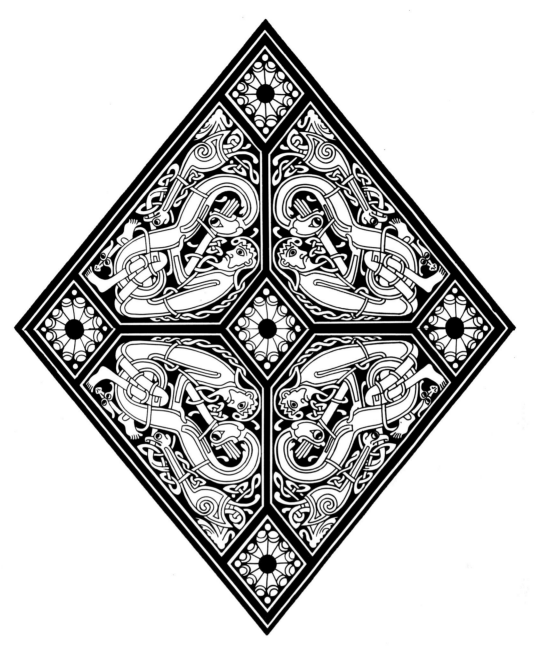

Mungo first built himself a hut from branches and twigs that the hound had gathered for him. In thanks for the creature's help he laid his hands on the hound's head and blessed him.

In the following months the hound would continually leave in search of other men, all of whom had also thought to build a monastery. He brought them back to join Mungo, and with the help of the robin and the hound each new arrival built himself a hut.

In a few years the small community that Mungo had started had grown into a monastery renowned for its generosity and kindness to the sick and to hungry travellers.

'Mungo, the Hound and the Robin' (1992)
man, dog and bird image adapted from the Book of Kells

St Patrick

Patrick was probably born around AD 395. At the age of sixteen he was carried off by raiders from his home, which was thought to be somewhere near the Severn estuary in Western Britain, and taken to Antrim in Ireland. Here he was forced to work as a herdsman for six years, before he found an opportunity to escape. It was during this time in Ireland that Patrick began to take religion seriously, and he spent long periods every day in intense prayer.

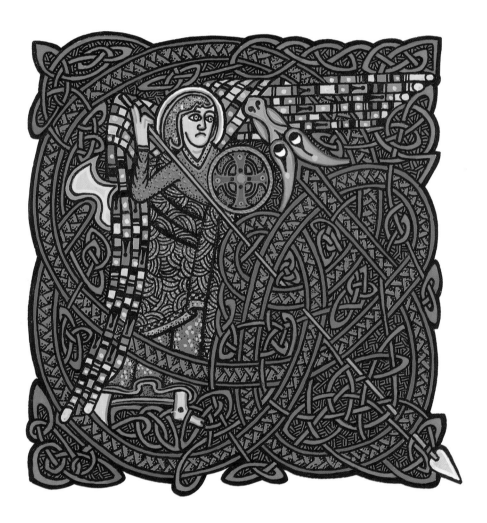

We are told that when he returned home Patrick had a dream in which he saw a man called Victoricus who handed him countless letters headed from the 'Voice of the Irish', imploring him to return to Ireland and to walk and preach amongst them.

For a time Patrick led a monastic existence on an island off the south coast. Then he trained for the priesthood in Gaul (France), in preparation for the task that lay ahead of him in Ireland.

'St Patrick' (1992)

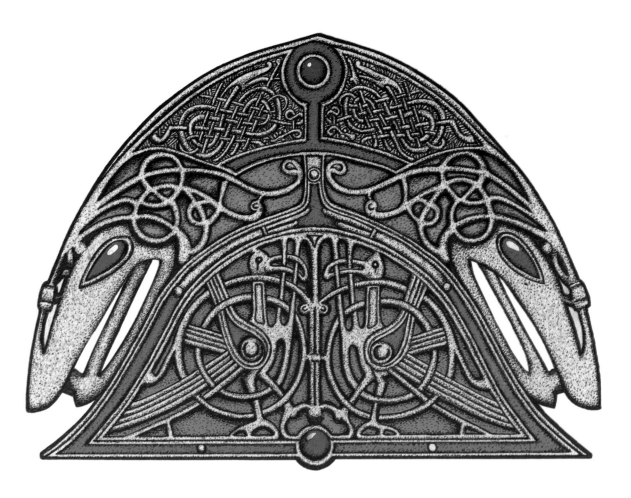

In AD 432 Patrick returned as bishop to an Ireland only partly Christianized; no great impression had been made on the pagan Irish chiefs or their tribes. At Tara in Meath, Laoghaire the High King of Ireland was celebrating the Sacred Spring Feast. No other fire was allowed to be lit whilst the ceremony was in progress. Far in the distance the druids saw points of light – fires lit by Patrick in celebration of Easter. They represented a direct challenge to the authority of the druids, who warned the King that if they were not put out now the Christian faith would take over and never die in Ireland.

Fifty years after Patrick's death, the Christianity he had brought with him had spread throughout Ireland.

In *Glastonbury and Her Saints*, The Revd Lionel Smithett Lewis puts forward the Somerset tradition that, after the completion of his missionary work, Patrick came to Glastonbury. Here he lived a blameless life, organizing and further developing a Celtic settlement near the Chalice Well. After his death he was buried at the right side of the altar in the old church. An ancient chapel dedicated to St Patrick still stands in the old Abbey grounds.

'St Patrick's Bell Shrine' (1992)
taken from the cast bronze original of AD 1100

119

St Columba and the Loch Ness Monster

The personality and achievements of Columba are chronicled in Adamann's *Life of St Columba*, one of the treasures of Celtic Christian history. It was written only twenty-seven years after the saint's death, and was based on conversations that Adamann had with men who had been Columba's monks.

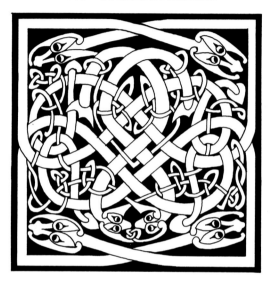

One story relates how, when the saint was travelling through the province of the Picts, he came upon a group of pagans burying one of their number near to the River Ness, where Columba needed to cross. The dead man's companions told Columba that, a while before, some aquatic monster had attacked their friend whilst he was swimming and that rescue came too late to save him.

On hearing this, Columba ordered one of his own companions to swim over to the other bank and bring back a boat that was beached there. Lugne Mocumin took off his clothes and dived into the water, but his movement across the surface of the water had not gone unnoticed by the monster, who was looking for new prey to sate his appetite. With a great rush the monster moved closer to the swimmer with its mouth wide open.

Everyone on the bank was terror-struck except Columba, who made a salutary sign of the Cross in the empty air and invoked the name of God. 'Go no further, nor touch the man,' Columba commanded. 'Go back at once.' The heathens marvelled as the terrified monster fled on hearing the words of the saint, and untouched and unharmed Lugne returned safely to the shore with the boat. The miracle which they had all witnessed magnified the God of the Christians.

'A Company of Serpents' (1992)

St Columba's Visitation

Whilst living in Iona, one day Columba assembled all the brethren and told them that he planned to go alone to the western plain of the island. No one was to follow him.

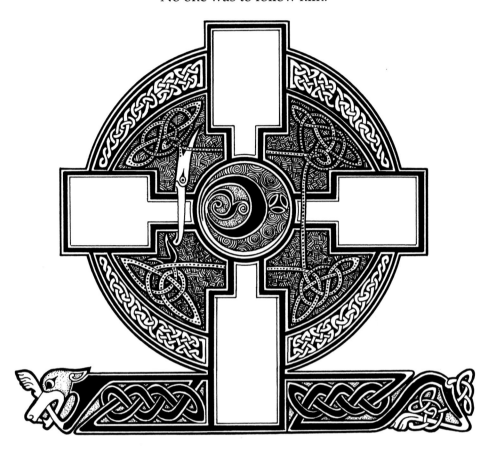

After Columba had left, one of the brothers who was over-curious set off in a different direction to find a vantage point from which he could observe the saint and discover the reason for his departure. He saw Columba on Sithean Mor – a great fairy mound – praying with his arms outstretched to Heaven. Then, looking up, he saw holy angels dressed in white descend from the sky and surround the holy man as he prayed.

The angels began to speak to Columba. Then, realizing they were being watched, they sped quickly back to the Heavens.

On his return, Columba once again assembled the brethren and enquired which of them had disobeyed his orders. The guilty brother, who was conscious of his disgraceful behaviour, begged forgiveness. Kneeling before Columba, the shamed brother promised never to reveal anything of the wondrous vision he had witnessed until after the death of the blessed man.

'Cross of Peace' (1992)

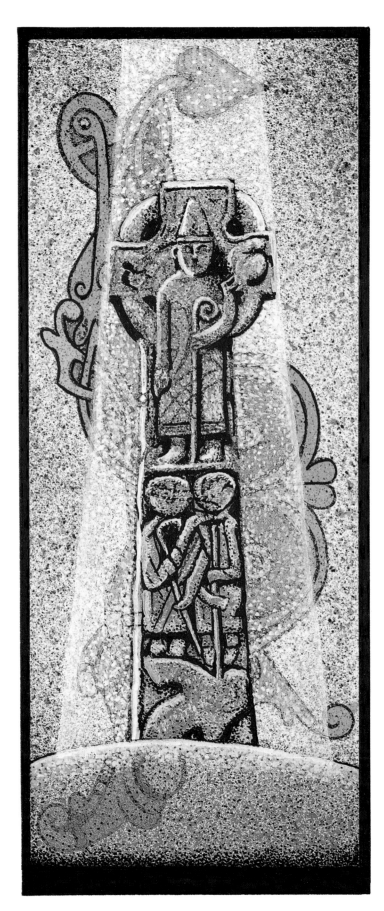

Standing Stones and Celtic Crosses

Before Christianity came to the shores of Britain numerous pagan standing stones were erected around the countryside. They were representations of the Tree of Life, the link between Heaven and Earth, and were probably used by the Celts to replace the sacred trees lost as a result of the early settlements and their agriculture.

Many stones were clearly phallic in shape, with a rounded top. Some were carved with basic patterns and were believed to be a source of potent energy that could be directed to the fertility of the earth in readiness for the next season's crops.

Some Celtic Christians noted the universal symbolism that was attached to the standing stones and found that in many ways it was compatible with their own teachings. Over a period of time they began to modify the stones with their own inscriptions, though some still show within the carvings the influence of a much older and pagan tradition.

'The Stone Cross' (1992)
based on the 12th century Doorty cross

'A Minute's Silence' (1985) ▶

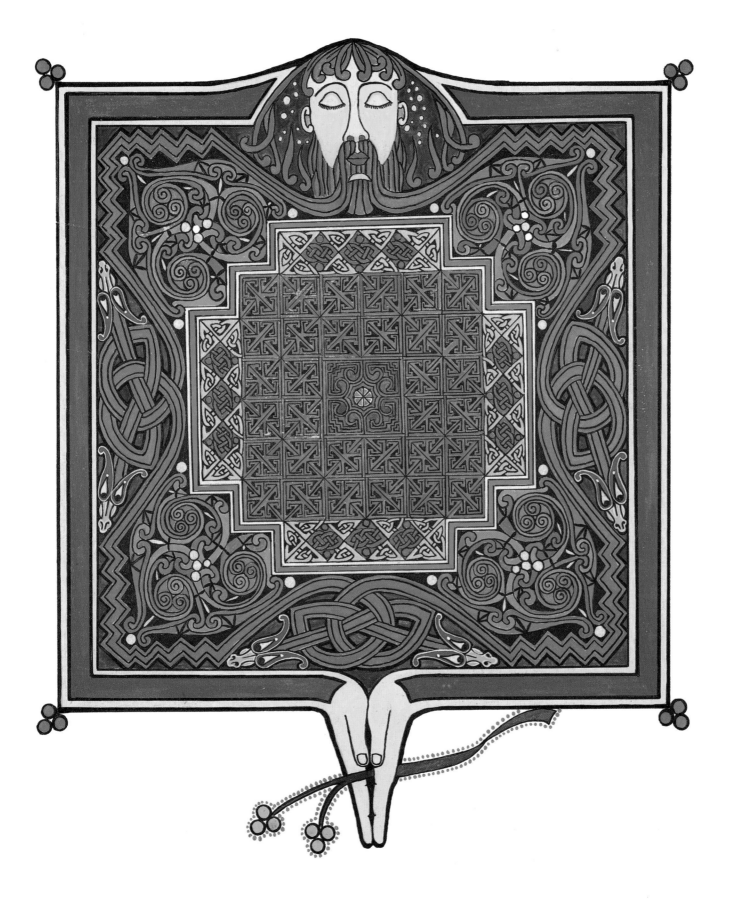

123

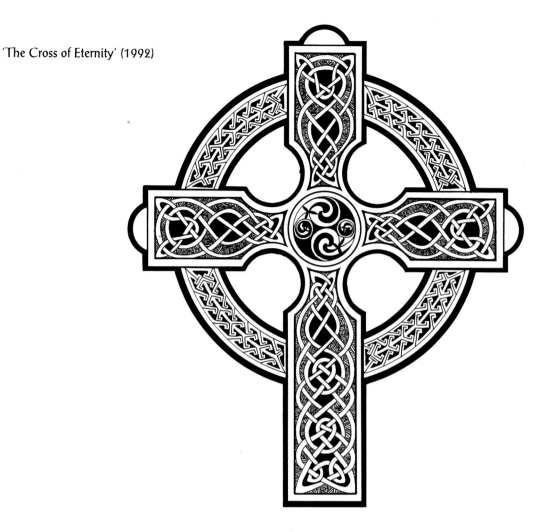

Celtic Cross

The Celtic cross is a magical symbol, and one that does not place Christianity at odds with its spiritual origins in the religious perceptions of man since the dawn of time.

Almost all civilizations in their early forms worshipped the Sun, which originally, amongst the Celts at least, seems to have been thought of as female. Around 1500 BC, with the fall of the Minoan goddess-based theocracy, the sexual polarity of western man's perception of the pantheon of the gods changed to one fundamentally male in character.

Amongst the Celts the symbolism of the Sun appears to have changed too. But they retained a balance, lost elsewhere in the West, between the archetypes of the male and female principles, which is equally present in the human psyche.

The circle represents wholeness, the round contours of the Earth, or female energy, and the cross represents the four directions of movement, or male energy, in the form of the winds, seasons and so on. So the two symbols superimposed express the 'both ways state' of being and becoming in harmony or balance.

The Celtic cross, then, is in effect a symbolic spiritual diagram, which is sometimes called a mandala. Across the face of the Earth such diagrams have appeared as the universal and essential symbols of integration, harmony and transformation. The circle is the original sign, the prime symbol of the nothing and the all, in which man finds and loses himself.

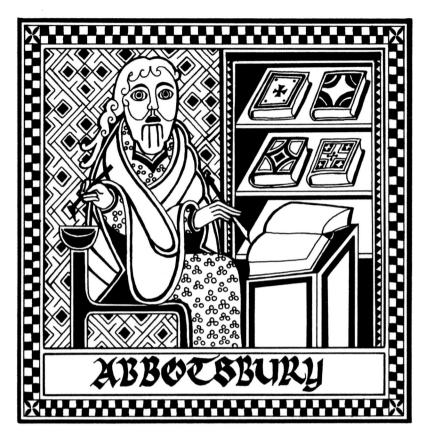

ABBOTSBURY

Illumination

The Celts' conversion to Christianity marks the emergence of a new phase of Celtic art, manuscript illumination, which gave artists the opportunity to create richly decorated masterpieces which would require the greatest skill.

Gerald of Wales wrote in the 12th century that he had seen in Kildare a manuscript that had 'intricacies so delicate and subtle, so exact and compact, so full of knots and links, with colours so fresh so vivid' that he regarded it as 'the work not of men, but of angels'. He tells a story of an angel appearing to the artist in a dream, showing him each design for him to memorize and copy when he awoke.

The understanding of the complex Christian mysteries and the significance of the pagan symbolism that is typical of much of Celtic illuminated art, such as in the Book of Kells, has been lost for centuries. Only now has its meaning, through intense study, began to re-emerge. The early Church absorbed a lot of the old tradition in its drive towards Christianizing the pagans, and their influence can be easily detected in the Book of Kells which contains images of severed heads, of humans with part animal forms and vice versa.

'Abbotsbury' (1992)

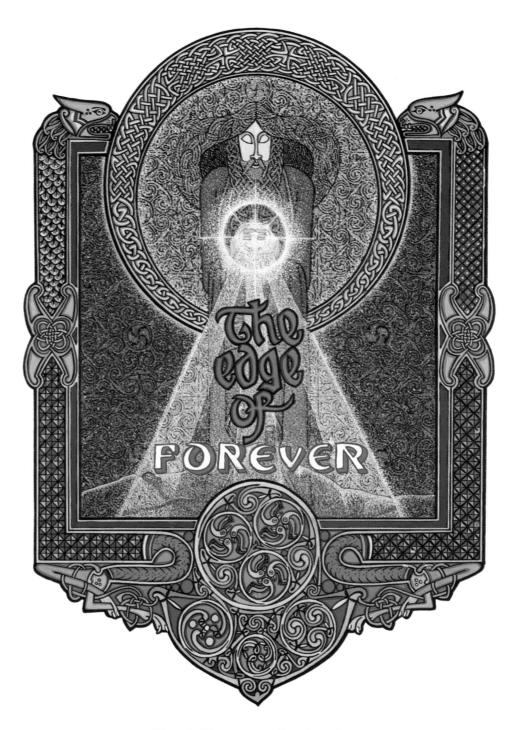

Time is like an ever-flowing river.
Past, present and future are mere moments along the journey.
Yet all are indelibly linked together –
Where one is, the others follow.
For today is just tomorrow's yesterday.

From *Merlin Awakes*

'The Edge of Forever' (1988)

Further Reading

Bamires, Steve, *The Irish Celtic Magical Tradition*, Aquarian, 1992

Bancroft, Anne, *Origins of the Sacred*, Penguin, 1987

Bryce, Derek, *Symbolism of the Celtic Cross*, Llanerch Enterprises, 1989

Carmichael, Alexander, *Carmina Gadelica*, Scottish Academic Press

Coghlan, Ronan, *The Encyclopedia of Arthurian Legends*, Element Books, 1992

Davis, Courtney, *Celtic Art of Courtney Davis*, Spirit of Celtia, 1985

Davis, Courtney, *The Celtic Art Source Book*, Blandford, 1985

Davis, Courtney, *Celtic Borders and Decoration*, Blandford, 1992

Davis, Courtney, *Celtic Designs and Motifs*, Dover Books, 1991

Eliade, M., *The Myth of the Eternal Return*, Princetown University Press, 1974

Laing, Lloyd and Jennifer, *Art of the Celts*, Thames and Hudson, 1992

Lewis, Lionel Smithett, *Glastonbury and Her Saints*, Thorsons, 1985

Matthews, John, *Taliesin*, Aquarian, 1991

Merry, Eleanor C., *The Flaming Door*, Floris Books, 1936

Paterson, Helena, and Davis, Courtney, *Celtic Tarot*, Aquarian, 1990

Pennick, Nigel, *Celtic Art in the Northern Tradition*, Nideck, 1992

Quiller, Peter, and Davis, Courtney, *Merlin Awakes*, Firebird Books, 1990

Quiller, Peter, and Davis, Courtney, *Merlin the Immortal*, Spirit of Celtia, 1987

Roberts, Forrester, and Davis, Courtney, *Symbols of the Grail Quest*, Spirit of Celtia, 1990

Rutherford, Ward, *The Druids*, Gordon and Cremonesi, 1978

Sharkey, John, *Celtic Mysteries*, Thames and Hudson, 1975

Spence, Lewis, *Magic Arts in Celtic Britain*, Aquarian, 1970

Stewart, R. J., *Celtic Gods, Celtic Goddesses*, Blandford, 1990

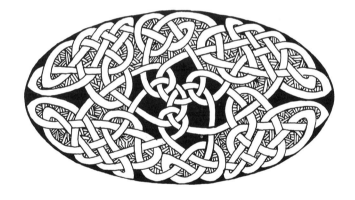

Index